JAMES

12
Inductive
Sessions
on
Practical
Christianity

BARRY SHAFER

www.zondervan.com

www.YouthSpecialties.com

Small Group Studies: James: 12 Inductive Sessions on Practical Christianity

Copyright © 2003 Youth Specialties

Youth Specialties Books, 300 South Pierce Street, El Cajon, California 92020, are published by Zondervan, 5300 Patterson Avenue Southeast, Grand Rapids, Michigan 49530

Library of Congress Cataloging-in-Publication Data

Shafer, Barry, 1961-
  James : 12 inductive sessions on practical Christianity / Barry Shafer.-- 1st ed.
        p. cm.
   ISBN 0-310-25166-4 (pbk.)
   1. Bible. N.T. James--Study and teaching. 2. Christian education of teenagers. I. Title.
BS2785.55.S52 2003
268'.433--dc21

                                                                    2003004900

Edited by Vicki Newby

Cover and interior design by Paz Design

Printed in the United States of America

03 04 05 06 07 / / 10 9 8 7 6 5 4 3 2 1

DEDICATION

This study is dedicated to you, the youth worker. You're taking a monumental step in helping your students experience something that's close to God's heart—his Word. And with the book of James, it's more than experiencing God's Word—it's doing it. I'm praying that you'll experience all the promises and blessings that come to those who know and do the Word of God.

ACKNOWLEDGMENTS

I'd like to extend a big thank you to the Zelos gang and to my wife, Dana, who have walked with me through the book of James, listened to me express my lapses in obedience as revealed through God's Word, and held me accountable in moving from expressing to doing.

CONTENTS

YOU MEAN I CAN KNOW GOD'S WILL?

As students cruise through their teen years, they begin to think about their lives as adults—their careers, who they will marry, what kinds of people they will become. For Christian teens, these thoughts ultimately lead to the million-dollar question: "What is God's will for my life?"

For youth workers who have the unique opportunity to guide students as they process this question, discovering the book of James and its practical applications in youth ministry is like striking gold. In this brief, five-chapter book, God makes it abundantly clear that we need not ask about his will concerning our lives. Instead, we can simply invest our lives in following the instructions he gave through his servant James. By doing James, we find ourselves doing God's will!

Looking to motivate students on leadership? Sacrifice? Godly behavior? Prayer? Sharing their faith? You've come to the right book. The book of James is so dense with instructions, commands, and imperatives that its pages should stick out of our Bibles as if made of cardboard. When it comes to our behavior and obedience, James isn't nebulous. Consequently, each group session in this study closes with an exercise designed to help students apply the message of James to their world right now.

This study does not examine James' letter verse-by-verse, but rather, teachable moment by teachable moment. You can take confidence in the fact that students will experience each of the author's major themes and be challenged to respond in light of these themes. And before long they'll know and do God's will.

Let's consider some background information for this entire book and then take a look at what's available to you in it.

How It Works

The number one prerequisite for teens who will participate in this study is spiritual curiosity—even a small amount! Of course, not every teen in your youth ministry is spiritually motivated or curious. For that reason, this study may not be for every student in your ministry.

But if you're like most youth workers, you probably know at least a handful of students who are ready to go deeper in their faith. These are the ones you'll want to invite to this study in James. Geared for small-group settings, each session includes some built-in Solitude—time students spend alone with God and his Word.

Where It Works

A home is the ideal setting for this study because of the relaxed, casual learning environment it creates. If you must meet in a church, we suggest you use a room or area that's different from your usual meeting space—perhaps a pastor's study, an office, or a chapel. The key is for students to experience a comfortable setting, yet one that encourages challenging study and discussion.

You should be aware of this logistical issue: during Solitude, your group members need to have room to spread out, to find personal space and some privacy with God. This doesn't mean your kids have to be in separate rooms. It may simply mean turning to face a wall or sitting behind a visual barrier like a plant or a couch. Be sure your teens know the limits—what areas to avoid and how close to stay to the meeting area.

What You Get

PREP IT

This is a guided personal study for the group leader. Because the most powerful teaching of God's Word flows out of the leader's personal experience in Scripture, you, the leader, need to spend ample time with Scripture before meeting with your group. You'll have plenty of space to write your thoughts and discoveries. Allow about an hour for personal study sometime before the session with your teens.

TEACH IT

This is the leader's cue sheet for leading the session. Teach It includes prompts and notes for moving the group through the exercises, as well as guidance for leading the group discussion. The following design elements will help you navigate through Teach It.

Some text is in normal type like what you're reading now. This font style indicates prompts to help the leader move from one exercise to the next within the session.

> ▸ *Type like this indicates questions or points of discussion to raise with your group. You may read these questions and comments word-for-word but you may be more comfortable reframing the questions and points in your own words so you can be more responsive to answers and other comments your students make.*

Type like this indicates suggested or sample responses.

Building trust

Two main factors facilitate interaction and sharing. First, you set the tone by being appropriately transparent. Your students don't expect you to be perfect—nor a complete failure for that matter—so don't be afraid to share about your struggles and successes. Of course some issues are inappropriate for leaders to mention to students, say, conflict among youth ministry leaders, even in the name of transparency.

Second, the level of sharing will never exceed the level of trust among the group members. If your students don't know each other well when you begin the study, it's appropriate to do some get-acquainted activities, at least for the first few weeks. And they need to feel safe from criticism and disrespect.

Many discussion questions ask students for personal opinions, experiences, applications, and assessments. Never force students to share. Ask for volunteers. Have sharing on a random basis rather than systematically moving through the group so students who choose not to contribute at certain points don't stand out.

Student Handouts

Each session has handouts for students to use during the session for study notes, journaling, and so forth. Students will need a folder or three-ring notebook to keep these in. Occasionally, the students will be asked to refer to sheets from previous sessions, so they should bring the notebook each week and add their copies of The Letter and the handouts. Permission to reproduce student handouts are granted only for buyer's own youth group. They can also be downloaded for free from www.YouthSpecialties.com/store/downloads (password: jimmy)

The Letter

The entire book of James can be found on pages 146-149. These reproducible pages are for your use when preparing for the session and for students' use during the session.

An integral part of this study is hands-on interaction with the text by marking key words, promises, instructions, and other phrases—which helps students observe important details that a casual reading might not uncover. Having bigger text and more space on this reproducible format facilitates this process.

Remember not to write on the originals in the book.

Use colored pencils to mark the text, so have a good supply available. Most sessions suggest having a couple of colors for each student. While not mandatory, students may find it helpful to use the same color or symbol (or both) from one session to the next when marking the same word or concept.

For example, a student may want to mark all references to God with a blue cloud. Another student may pick a different color but use the same symbol.

Symbols are usually suggested, but you may want to ask your group for their suggestions.

Prayer Partners

The purpose of this study is not to fill up the next 12 Wednesday nights in your students' youth ministry schedule. It's an opportunity for God to speak to your teens through his Word. Therefore, the most important component of your preparation is prayer. We suggest that you organize a group of prayer partners—adults in your student ministry or church—who will pray specifically for your group's experience in the book of James.

Give these prayer partners the names of your group members, the time frame of the study, and any information that will help them pray specifically for you and your students. In fact, take five minutes now to gather the names and phone numbers of people who have an active prayer life and a heart for the students in your ministry. Then take another 10 minutes to call them, asking them to pray.

What You'll Need

For every session, you'll need the same basic materials: Bibles, pens, colored pencils, a whiteboard and markers, and copies of The Letter and student handouts.

Some sessions have options that need a few other supplies. Session 8 has an optional worship time that requires a little extra preparation time, and the format of Session 11 is different from other sessions, so some advanced planning is necessary.

Although a whiteboard is suggested throughout, you can substitute a flip chart, butcher paper taped to the wall, or whatever works conveniently for you.

THE JAMES GANG
James 1

SESSION
1

THE
JAMES
GANG

JAMES 1

PREP IT PREP IT PREP IT PREP IT PREP IT PREP IT

You're about to spend time doing one of the most important things you can today: preparing to lead teens in a study of God's Word. For the next hour (the estimated amount of preparation time) everything else can wait.

There's a strong possibility—actually, a promise—that the Lord wants to say something to you and your students through the book of James. God promised a reward beyond anything we can imagine when we spend the kind of time with him that he requires. But don't take my word for it; take his. Before you dive into James, take a moment to soften your heart and clear your mind to hear God's voice. As you read Proverbs 2:1-11 below, note the intense action—the kind of time God asks for when it comes to his Word. Then find the payoff that's promised as a result.

My son, if you accept my words and store up my commands within you, turning your ear to wisdom and applying your heart to understanding, and if you call out for insight and cry aloud for understanding, and if you look for it as for silver and search for it as for hidden treasure, then you will understand the fear of the Lord and find the knowledge of God.

For the Lord gives wisdom, and from his mouth come knowledge and understanding. He holds victory in store for the upright, he is a shield to those whose walk is blameless, for he guards the course of the just and protects the way of his faithful ones. Then you will understand what is right and just and fair—every good path. For wisdom will enter your heart, and knowledge will be pleasant to your soul. Discretion will protect you, and understanding will guard you.
—Proverbs 2:1-11

What an incredible payoff! And aren't the promises in this passage—finding the knowledge of God, understanding every good path, being protected by discretion—benefits you want in your life and the lives of your students?

Yet how consistently do we actually do what God asks for in these verses? Perhaps your study in James can be a step toward storing up, crying out for, looking for and applying the Word of God. As you study James, not only will you be impacted by the message of this book, but you'll also enjoy the rewards God promises for taking his Word seriousl

SEARCH

Will the real James please stand?

There's a reasonable chance you know a few things about the book of James. Perhaps that's why you chose this study. But let's start from scratch, assuming we know nothing about who wrote the book and why. Even if you already know this info, your students probably don't. You could simply tell them what you know, but they'd miss the reward of discovering it for themselves. Your group will benefit from digging for the information on their own—and incidentally, so will you.

The New Testament mentions several men named James. Read the passages below, and record the identity or description of each James.

WILL THE REAL JAMES
PLEASE STAND?

Matthew 10:2-4   Matthew 13:54-58   James 1:1

PERSON	INDENTITY/ DESCRIPTION	NEW INFO
JAMES A		
JAMES B		
JAMES C		
JAMES, THE AUTHOR		

Is this enough information to conclude who wrote the book of James? Probably not. Here's where a few other Scriptures can help us out. As the church matured in the years following Jesus' resurrection, several people emerged as leaders. You probably know of Peter, Paul, and John, but a key leader who didn't get as much press was James.

As you read the following passages, write down the new information you learn (or can reasonably infer) about any person named James. If you're able to determine which James the verse refers to, write the facts in the New Info column next to the appropriate name. If you can't correlate the information to a specific person, write it in the fourth column.

ACTS 1:12-14
This took place just after Jesus left the earth to be with the Father.

ACTS 12:1-2

ACTS 15:12-23
This was the world's first church board meeting. The apostles, elders, and church leaders met in Jerusalem to decide whether Gentiles should become Jews (and undergo circumcision) before they become Christians.

ACTS 21:17-19
This scene describes Paul's arrival in Jerusalem after his three missionary journeys.

1 CORINTHIANS 15:1-8

GALATIANS 1:13-19; 2:7-10

BACKGROUND

You say disciple; I say apostle

It may help you to know that men other than Jesus' 12 original disciples were referred to in Scripture as apostles. Barnabas and Paul are both called apostles (Acts 14:14); Paul also writes in 1 Corinthians 15 that Jesus was seen by "the Twelve" and "then by all the apostles." Based on these "apostle sightings" in Scripture, when the Bible refers to James as an apostle, it doesn't necessarily refer to one of Jesus' original 12 disciples.

Cast your vote

Do you see a particular James emerging as a strong candidate as author of the book of James? Here are some key points you may have gathered so far:

— James, the brother of John, is an unlikely candidate since he was killed before the book of James could have been written (Acts 12).

— One James definitely emerged as a pillar (elder and apostle) of the first-century church. This James was a minister to the Jews (Acts 15; Acts 21; 1 Corinthians 15; Galatians 2). James 1:1 indicates that the author was addressing a Jewish audience.

— Jesus' half brother James emerged as a pillar (elder and apostle) of the first-century church (Acts 1; Galatians 1).

Who do you think authored the book of James?

❏ James, brother of John, son of Zebedee

❏ James, son of Alphaeus

❏ James, the half brother of Jesus

If you checked James, the half brother of Jesus, you agree with the most widely held conclusion regarding the authorship of the New Testament book of James.

Now that's a conversion!

Read John 7:1-5 for another piece of information to throw into the mix. What do you learn about Jesus' brothers?

_____

_____

If Jesus' half brother James was included in this scene (and we have no reason to think he wasn't), he's made a big leap from nonbeliever to author of a New Testament letter! But isn't that just like God? Take a minute to reflect on the experiences that would have made a difference in James' life by reviewing the Scripture passages you just studied. Write down two or three experiences that may have contributed to James' conversion.

_____

_____

How can these same things make a difference in your life?

_____

_____

What hope does this give you for the nonbelievers in your life?

_____

_____

How can you help nonbelievers experience the same things James experienced?

_____

_____

Being a Christian wasn't easy then, either

Now that we have a feel for who wrote the book of James, we can better understand why he wrote it-and the better we understand the context of a book (including the reason it was written) the more accurately and powerfully we can apply God's message.

Using The Letter, read the first chapter of James. As you read, underline any clues about James' audience and what they were facing. It may help you to know that James often introduced a new subject with the phrase "my brothers."

By examining the situations James addressed, we can get a good picture of what his readers were experiencing. Looking back at what you underlined in James 1, take a minute to list in the first column anything James' readers appear to have been facing, based on problems and situations addressed in the chapter. You'll use the second column shortly.

James' readers	Your students
_____	_____
_____	_____
_____	_____

Based on what you've discovered in James 1, what do you think was James' purpose for writing this letter? What was he trying to get across to his readers?

_____

_____

Who did James write to?

Your students may wonder about James' reference to his readers: "To the twelve tribes scattered among the nations." Who were these people? The phrase "twelve tribes" is a reference to the Old Testament tribes of Israel. The phrase "scattered among the nations" comes from the Greek word *diaspora*, which is used to describe Jewish people living outside Palestine. However, there are several schools of thought concerning James' specific audience. Here are three possibilities:

— James was writing to Jewish Christians who lived outside of Palestine and were scattered because of persecution.

— James' intended audience was the true people of God—Jewish and Gentile believers—living in the last days.

— James was writing to all Christians who must now live in this physical world, separated from their true homeland in heaven.

In his letter, James makes several references familiar to Jewish Christians (James 1:24-25; 2:2; 2:8-13; 2:19; 4:11-12). Other New Testament passages refer to this group in a similar way (for example, Acts 11:19). Plus, as you'll see in James' letter, he's a practical guy—not one to get too metaphorical. So the most literal option is probably the most accurate. The most likely conclusion is the first option—Jewish Christians who lived outside of Palestine.

APPLICATION
Connecting parallel worlds

After you've listed the information about James' readers, take a few minutes to draw some parallels between his audience and your students. What are some specific situations your students are facing that are parallel to what James' readers were facing? Write your thoughts in the second column of the chart above. Be sure to include the names of your students when you describe the situations. In fact, take a minute to ask the Holy Spirit to bring to mind trials, temptations, and other challenges your students are facing.

REFLECTION
James: a profile

Let's put it all together by reflecting on the faith journey of James, the brother of Jesus.

What are some reasons why he was well suited to address these issues with the "twelve tribes scattered among the nations"?

_____

_____

Based on what you've observed in James 1, how would you describe James' concern for his readers?

_____

_____

What do you think motivated his concern?

_____

_____

How would you describe the relationship James had with his readers?

_____

_____

How does this relationship compare to the relationship you have with your students?

_____

_____

What are some ways you could be more of a James to your students?

_____

_____

How can you encourage your students to be more of a James to the people around them?

_____

_____

What do you make of the fact that James didn't identify himself as a brother of Jesus? (Talk about a way to have instant credibility!) Compare the claims he could have made to the way he presented himself in his letter.

_____

_____

Before you close this book, read through Teach It for this lesson so you're familiar with it. You'll need to choose one of the closing options. Pray for your session and for the students God is drawing to this study.

SESSION 1

THE JAMES GANG
James 1

■ OPENING

This exercise is intended to get students thinking about the book of James and acquaints them with the author and recipients of this letter.

■ SEARCH

Will the real James please stand?

Students will discover for themselves which James of the New Testament most likely wrote the book of James.

■ APPLICATION

Now that's a conversion!

Students will discover surprise information about the author of James and apply it to their personal faith journeys.

■ SEARCH

Being a Christian wasn't easy then, either

Students will see issues addressed in James 1 and make comparisons to the issues they face today.

■ CLOSING

Pass it on

This option gives students a chance to discuss the James-type relationships in their lives.

YOU'LL NEED

a whiteboard and markers

Bibles

pens

copies of The James Gang (pages 13-14), one for each student

copies of The Letter—James 1 (page 146), one for each student

colored pencils

postage-paid postcards (optional)

If your students don't know each other well, plan to do ice breakers for several weeks.

OPENING

To help students change their focus to the lesson, begin with a brief comment something like this:

▸ *God has something specific he wants to teach us from the book of James. For this session and every other time we gather, I'd like us to imagine being completely separated from the busyness and stress of the day and to focus only on the things in this room—things like God's Word, God's Spirit, and each other.*

▸ *What specifics can we pray for to help you maximize your experience in the book of James?*

You may want to pray that students will see through the deceptions that Satan will throw their way to distract them from their study of James such as being busy or tired.

After prayer begin with this brainstorming exercise.

> ▶ *Off the top of your head, tell me everything you know about the book of James.*

List their responses on the board. Be sure to write down everything the students say, including responses like, "The title is James." If they don't have any other ideas, acknowledge it and encourage them with the thought that the situation will soon change.

> *Read James 1:1 and tell me two things:*
>
> ▶ *Who wrote the book of James?*
> ▶ *Who were the first readers of the book?*

Write their responses on the board. Have students write the same information on their handouts, The James Gang (pages 13-14). Students may have a question about "the twelve tribes scattered among the nations." Share some background on this subject from your session prep.

> ▶ *Do you know of anyone else in Scripture named James besides the author of James?*

Even if they answer no, use this question to let your students know there was more than one James in the New Testament.

> ▶ *Can we tell from James 1:1 which James wrote this book?*

Will the real James please stand?

Since you want your students to search the Bible for information and not just have it handed to them, explain the benefit they will receive by doing it themselves:

> ▶ *We could read a note from one of our Bibles and find out which James was the most likely author of this Bible book, but we can also dig it out on our own. And if we dig the information out ourselves, we'll learn a lot more about the author and better understand the message God has for us in the book of James.*

Invite the group to spend a few minutes gathering information about three New Testament men named James—all potential authors of the book. Direct them to the next section of this week's handout. While the students are doing this research, reproduce the basic framework of the chart on the board. Here's about what you'll have on the chart when the discussion is finished.

SMALL GROUP STUDIES: JAMES
12 INDUCTIVE SESSIONS ON PRACTICAL CHRISTIANITY

WILL THE REAL JAMES
PLEASE STAND?

Matthew 10:2-4 ▪ Matthew 13:54-58 ▪ James 1:1

PERSON	IDENTITY/ DESCRIPTION	NEW INFO
JAMES A	*James, an apostle, son of Zebedee, brother of John*	*This James was killed by Herod (Acts 12:2).*
JAMES B	*James, an apostle, son of Alphaeus*	*This James was part of the inner circle after Jesus' ascension. He constantly joined others in prayer (Acts 1:14).*
JAMES C	*James, half brother of Jesus*	*This James was a leader in the church, and Paul noted he was an apostle (Galatians 1:13-19).*
JAMES, THE AUTHOR	*James, a servant of Jesus*	

GENERAL JAMES INFO

The James in Acts 15 was a church leader; his contribution led to this council's final conclusion (Acts 15:12-23).

This James is portrayed as a vital church leader who was headquartered in Jerusalem (Acts 21:17-19).

Jesus made a post-resurrection appearance to a James who wasn't one of the Twelve (1 Corinthians 15:1-8).

This James, Jesus' brother, was a pillar in the church and a minister to the Jews (Galatians 1:13-19; 2:7-10).

After about 10 minutes, call the group members back together.

▸ *What did you find out about each of the Jameses you read about?*

▸ *Can we tell from this information which James wrote the book of James?*

▸ *Since we can't be sure of the author based on these verses, let's look at some other verses that can give us some help here. Read the next six passages listed on the handout and write down your insights. If you're able to determine which James the verse is referring to, write the facts of the passage in the New Info column next to the description of that James. If you can't correlate the information to a specific person, write it in the General James Info column.*

Allow your students about 10 minutes to work and then gather them together. Work as a group to add the new information to the chart on the board. You may also want to help them figure out these additional ideas that may not be so obvious.

— Since the James in Acts 21 is headquartered in Jerusalem, he probably ministered to Jewish Christians.

— While Paul doesn't identify the James in chapter 2 as Jesus' brother, that's probably who he was referring to since he had just referred to him in the previous chapter.

▶ *Which James seems to be the most likely author of James?*

▶ *How can we be fairly certain that this James is the author?*

Elicit the conclusion that the half brother of Jesus is the most probable author. This is the most widely held conclusion among Bible scholars—folks who keep track of this type of information. The main points to support this choice include-

— James, the brother of John, was taken off the list of candidates early; he was killed before he could have authored the book (Acts 12).

— One man named James definitely emerged as a pillar (elder and apostle) of the first-century church; he was a minister to the Jews (Acts 15; Acts 21; 1 Corinthians 15; Galatians 2).

— Jesus' half brother James definitely emerged as a pillar (elder and apostle) of the first-century church (Acts 1; Galatians 1).

Now feel free to invite the students to check the footnotes or study notes in their Bibles on this point.

APPLICATION

Now that's a conversion!

Ask one student to slowly read John 7:1-5 aloud. Ask the rest of the group to write down whatever they learn about Jesus' brothers (which would have included James) as the passage is being read. Point your students to the next section on their handout.

After the student finishes, ask questions along these lines:

▶ *What do we learn about James in these verses?*

▶ *What change do we see in James from early in his life to later?*

▶ *What does this teach you about God?*

▶ *What does this teach you about yourself?*

At one time James didn't believe his half brother was the Son of God, yet later he was a leader in the church and wrote a book of the Bible. God can save anyone. He can and will use anyone to do great things for him. The past doesn't matter to God. No matter what I've done in my past, I'm not disqualified from being used by God in a great way.

SEARCH

Being a Christian wasn't easy then, either

▶ *Now that we have some background on James the author, we can better understand James the book. We're going to use the first chapter to help us understand James' purpose for writing this letter. Find a spot where you can have a little privacy—at least visually or mentally. Take the next 10 minutes to read James 1. As you read, underline anything James' readers were experiencing.*

After several minutes, regroup and ask this question:

▸ *Based on the first chapter, what issues do you think James' readers were facing?*

Many kinds of trials
Lack of wisdom
Humble circumstances
Temptation
Angry people
Moral filth, evil
Slanderous talk

Record the students' responses on the board. Have your students write the ideas on their handouts also.

▸ *Take a moment to circle three issues mentioned by James that are similar to issues you're facing right now. Think about your friends. Write down names of your friends beside issues they are facing.*

▸ *Based on what you've seen in James 1, why do you think James wrote this letter?*

▸ *How does this purpose apply to you and the issues you're facing in your life?*

▸ *James cared deeply about the people he was writing to, and he wanted to encourage them in their faith. What are some ways you can be a James to the friends whose names you wrote on your sheet?*

If time allows, you may want to ask for volunteers to share the topics they circled on their lists.

CLOSING

Pass it on

▸ *Under God's inspiration, James was moved to help followers of Christ—the 12 scattered tribes— face the many trials and issues in their lives. I'd like you to think in two directions:*

▸ *Who is a James to you—someone who's helping you with your faith and encouraging you to do well?*

▸ *Who's someone you can be a James to—someone you can enourage and help?*

▸ *Take a minute to list any names that come to mind.*

Give the students a minute or two to respond. Then ask any volunteers to share their thoughts. Close the session by challenging the students to make contact this week with the people they listed, thanking the Jameses in thier lives and taking action to be a James to someone else. You may want to supply them with stamped postcards to facilitate the contact. Close the session in prayer.

THE JAMES GANG
James 1

OPENING

What do we learn about the author and recipients of this letter in James 1:1?

Author

_____

_____

First Readers

_____

_____

SEARCH

Will the real James please stand?

The New Testament mentions several men named James. Read the three passages below and write what you learn about each James (there are four) in the column labeled Identity/Description. We'll get to the other two columns in a minute.

WILL THE REAL JAMES
PLEASE STAND?
Matthew 10:2-4 n Matthew 13:54-58 n James 1:1

PERSON	INDENTITY/ DESCRIPTION	NEW INFO
JAMES A		
JAMES B		
JAMES C		
JAMES, THE AUTHOR		

Read the following six passages. Write down your insights. If you're able to determine which James the verse is referring to, write the facts of the passage in the New Info column next to the description of that James. If you can't correlate the information to a specific person, write it in the General James Info column.

ACTS 1:12-14
This took place just after Jesus left the earth to be with the Father.

ACTS 12:1-2

ACTS 15:12-23

This was the world's first church board meeting. The apostles, elders, and church leaders met in Jerusalem to decide whether Gentiles should become Jews before they become Christians.

ACTS 21:17-19

This scene, which describes Paul's arrival in Jerusalem after his three missionary journeys, took place within 30 years of Jesus' resurrection and ascension.

1 CORINTHIANS 15:1-8

GALATIANS 1:13-19; 2:7-10

APPLICATION
Now that's a conversion!

What do you learn about Jesus' brothers from John 7:1-5?

_____

_____

SEARCH
Who did James write to?

What issues mentioned in James 1 were James' readers facing?

_____

_____

CLOSING
Focus on Relationships

Who is a James to you—someone who's helping you with your faith and encouraging you to do well?

_____

_____

Who's someone you can be a James to—someone you can encourage and help with his or her faith?

_____

_____

DO YOU HAVE ISSUES?

James 1:1-18

No one—not God, not Jesus, not the Holy Spirit—ever said that the Christian life would be easy. In fact, the Bible tells us we can expect quite the opposite. As you prepare your heart to study James 1—a chapter warning us to expect trials—read some words from Jesus that give insight into how to endure life's difficulties. Watch for what Jesus says to do and the payoff for doing it.

Therefore everyone who hears these words of mine and puts them into practice is like a wise man who built his house on the rock. The rain came down, the streams rose, and the winds blew and beat against that house; yet it did not fall, because it had its foundation on the rock. But everyone who hears these words of mine and does not put them into practice is like a foolish man who built his house on sand. The rain came down, the streams rose, and the winds blew and beat against that house, and it fell with a great crash.

—Matthew 7:24-27

SEARCH

What do you find here?

In Session 1 we glanced at the various situations addressed in James 1. You may have noticed that with each challenging situation, James included some encouragement for his readers. Looking at the situations you've marked on The Letter—James 1 (these are noted in the left-hand column below), circle any encouragement or instructions James gave concerning them. Then write them in the right-hand column:

PROBLEM	ENCOURAGEMENT OR INSTRUCTIONS
TRIALS (1:2)	
LACK OF WISDOM (1:5)	
HUMBLE CIRCUMSTANCES (1:9)	
TEMPTATION (1:13)	

REFLECTION

You want me to do what?!

From the looks of it, things weren't going so well for James' readers. They were bombarded with trials, their circumstances were humble, and on top of it all, they were dogged by temptation. Sounds like a day in the life of a student—or even a youth leader—doesn't it?

So how about you? How have you been handling your trials, life circumstances, and temptations? Take a moment to put yourself in the place of James' readers.

In the first section below, write anything you're facing that parallels what James' audience must have been facing.

Based on James 1, in the second section write how you're instructed to respond to these problems. In the third section write why you're encouraged to respond that way.

Problem

1. What trials are you facing right now? (If life's great at the moment, answer this: What trials are you afraid to face?)

_____

_____

2. In what areas do you lack wisdom or feel deficient and inadequate?

_____

_____

3. How do you feel about your life status and circumstances?

_____

_____

4. What are your major areas of temptation? (Write in code if you prefer.)

_____

How to respond?

1. _____

_____

2. _____

_____

3. _____

_____

4. _____

_____

SESSION

2

DO YOU
HAVE
ISSUES?

JAMES
1:1-18

(Read carefully and you'll find at least one reason for each situation.)

1. _____

_____

2. _____

_____

3. _____

_____

4. _____

_____

There's a good chance that you identify with one of these situations more than the others. Scripture is packed with teaching and encouragement on all four situations, but for the next exercise, choose one or two that resonate most with you. (You'll be asking your students to choose two.)

With each situation, you'll be asked what you can change—right now—to respond to it the way the Lord asks you to. Here are some guidelines to use in responding:

— Be specific. Write down specific actions you can take within the next 24 hours.

— Be prayerful. Ask the Holy Spirit what he's anxious to say to you concerning this subject.

— Be intentional. Don't gloss over this exercise. Use it as an opportunity to show God that you're serious about obeying his Word.

Trials

As you read the following passages, look for answers to these questions:

— What types of trials are described?   — What are the rewards for standing firm?

— What encouragement is given?

MATTHEW 5:10-12   *1 PETER 1:6-9*

_____   _____

_____   _____

JOHN 16:33   *2 CORINTHIANS 1:3-7*

_____   _____

HEBREWS 10:32-38

_____

_____

The verses you just read are packed with rewards for those who stand firm through the rough stuff. How can these rewards motivate you to "consider it pure joy" when you face trials of many kinds?

_____

_____

_____

_____

Lacking Wisdom

As you read the next three passages, look for the following information:

— What is the context of the passage?

— What do you learn about God?

— What parallels do you see between this situation and James 1?

1 KINGS 3:6-14   *DANIEL 2:19-23*

_____   _____

_____   _____

DANIEL 1:17-21

_____

_____

What changes do you need to make in order to receive wisdom as Solomon and Daniel did?

_____

_____

Humble Circumstances

As you read the next four passages, write down what God's people are to focus on.

MATTHEW 23:11-12   *1 TIMOTHY 6:7-11*

_____   _____

PHILIPPIANS 4:11-13   *HEBREWS 13:5-6*

SESSION
2

DO YOU
HAVE
ISSUES?

JAMES
1:1-18

What adjustments do you need to make in order to pursue the things of God (which may lead to humble circumstances) rather than the things of the world (which may lead to comfortable—even luxurious—circumstances)?

Temptation

As you read the following passages, look for the answers to these questions:

— What's the root of temptation?

— What are the consequences of caving in to temptation?

— What can give you strength to beat temptation?

GENESIS 3:1-7   *HEBREWS 2:17-3:1*

2 CORINTHIANS 12:7-10   *JAMES 1:13-15*

Write down three observations from these verses—things to do or ways to think—that can help you conquer temptation.

CLOSING

You too can keep from falling!

Do you have issues? Fortunately God doesn't leave us to our own devices as we navigate the challenges life throws our way. In fact, if we'd just follow the instructions James gives and trust the encouragement he offers, we'd be like the wise man Jesus described in Matthew 7: we wouldn't fall.

Before wrapping up today's study, take a few minutes to read Teach It for this lesson.

You'll need to choose an application option and collect the appropriate materials ahead of time. They aren't difficult to locate, but you'll need some extra time.

DO YOU HAVE ISSUES?
James 1:1-18

SESSION

2

DO YOU
HAVE
ISSUES?

JAMES
1:1-18

■ OPENING

Distribute materials and open with prayer.

■ SEARCH

What do you find here?

Students will see that, accompanying the issues raised in Session 1, James provides instructions to help navigate the hardships as well as encouragement to endure them.

■ SOLITUDE

Make it personal

Students will choose two issues from James 1 to personally investigate on a deeper level.

■ APPLICATION

C-clamps and solitude

This option provides an opportunity for students to share Wow! moments and commitments from their solitude time.

■ CLOSING

You too can keep from falling!

YOU'LL NEED

a whiteboard and markers

Bibles

pens

copies of Do You Have Issues (pages 25-27), one for each student

copies of The Letter—James 1 (page 146), one for each new student

colored pencils

C-clamp or locking pliers, dictionary, penny, fishing lure (optional)

index cards (optional)

Students who were present for the last session should use the copies of The Letter: James 1 they have already marked.

After the students have gathered, distribute materials and give them a quiet minute to make a mental break from their busy day. Open the session with prayer. Check in with your teens about how they're doing on applications from the last session.

What do you find here?

Write on the board the four key issues faced by James' readers, which were uncovered in Session 1: trials, lack of wisdom, humble circumstances, and temptation. Leave space to write beneath each issue.

> ▸ *At the end of Session 1, we uncovered four issues that James' readers were facing: trials, lack of wisdom, humble circumstances, and temptation. As James writes about each issue, he also gives his readers encouragement and instructions. Read James 1:1-18 using your copy of The Letter. As you read, draw a circle around anything you would consider an encouragement in facing these issues. Draw a box around any instructions related to these issues.*

After about five minutes (or when most have finished), draw your students' attention to the board.

> ▸ *Look at the instructions you drew boxes around. According to James, how are we asked to respond to these issues?*

Write the responses beneath the corresponding issues on the board and ask the students to write the info in the spaces provided on their handout.

Trials

Consider it pure joy (1:2).

Humble circumstances

Take pride in your high position (1:9).

Lack of wisdom

Ask God for wisdom (1:5).

Temptations

Don't blame God for the temptation (1:13).

> ▸ *Take a couple of minutes to list two or three personal examples from each category that you're facing right now.*

After a few minutes ask for volunteers to share their examples.

> ▸ *James' instructions tell us how we're to respond to these issues. His words of encouragement tell us why we're to respond this way. Look at the phrases of encouragement you've circled and explain why we're to respond to these issues the way James told us to.*

Add this information to the board and ask your teens to add it to their handouts.

Trials

I'm being matured, so that I won't be lacking anything (1:4).

Lack of wisdom

God wants to give wisdom generously, without finding fault (1:5).

Humble circumstances

The rich will pass away like a wildflower (1:10).

Temptations

Every good and perfect gift comes from God, who doesn't change (1:17).

We are born through the word of truth and are the firstfruits of all God created (1:18).

SOLITUDE
Make it personal

▸ *There's a good chance you identify with one of these issues more than the others. In this next exercise, I want to give you an opportunity to experience more teaching and encouragement on whatever your issue is.*

▸ *Take a minute to choose two issues you'd like to know more about.*
Now take your Bible and handout, and move to a place of solitude. Follow the remainder of instructions on your handout, and open your heart and mind to all that God wants to teach you.

APPLICATION
C-clamps and solitude

Use the following items to represent the four issues in James 1:

— a C-clamp or a set of locking pliers (trials)

— a dictionary (lack of wisdom)

— a penny or an empty wallet (humble circumstances)

— a fishing lure (temptations)

After about 10 minutes of solitude, call the group back together and have them form a circle. Put the visual aids in the middle of the circle. Ask for student volunteers to choose an issue they'd like to share about. Give them the option of using a visual aid to illustrate their issues. Ask students to share Wow! moments they experienced during their time alone with God and any commitments they made.

When the students have finished sharing, encourage them to find one of these items at home—or pick one up at a store—and put it in a conspicuous place where they'll see it often. (They may even want to decorate it.) They can use the item as a reminder of the changes they've committed to make.

You too can keep from falling!

Ask a volunteer to close the session with prayer. The students may want to pray specifically about the issues the group discussed.

DO YOU HAVE ISSUES?

James 1:1-18

SESSION
2

DO YOU
HAVE
ISSUES?

JAMES
1:1-18

SEARCH

What do you find here?

In the second column list the instructions James gives us in chapter 1 about how are we asked to respond to each issue.

In the third column list two or three personal examples you're facing right now for each issue.

In the fourth column, list James' words of encouragement in chapter 1 about why we're to respond as he instructs.

PROBLEM	HOW TO RESPOND?	PERSONAL EXAMPLES	WHY RESPOND THIS WAY?
TRIALS			
LACK OF WISDOM			
HUMBLE CIRCUMSTANCES			
TEMPTATIONS			

SOLITUDE

Make it personal

Trials

As you read the following passages, look for answers to these questions:

— What types of trials are described?

— What encouragement is given?

— What are the rewards for standing firm in each trial?

MATTHEW 5:10-12

_____

_____

1 PETER 1:6-9

_____

_____

JOHN 16:33

_____

_____

2 CORINTHIANS 1:3-7

_____

_____

HEBREWS 10:32-38

_____

_____

How do you tend to react to difficult situations in your life?

❏ I ask, "Why me?"

❏ I ask, "Why did God let this happen?"

❏ I tend to reject God.

❏ I wouldn't call it pure joy, but I grit my teeth and bear it.

❏ I consider it pure joy, knowing God has a plan.

The passages you just read promise some awesome rewards to those who stand firm through rough stuff. How can these rewards motivate you to "consider it pure joy" when you face trials of many kinds? Write your thoughts below.

_____

Lacking Wisdom

As you read the next three passages, look for the following information:

— What do you learn about God?

— What similarities do you see between these passages about wisdom and the verses you read in James?

1 KINGS 3:6-14

_____

_____

DANIEL 2:19-23

_____

_____

DANIEL 1:17-21

SESSION

2

DO YOU
HAVE
ISSUES?

JAMES
1:1-18

When you feel inadequate for a task or face a big decision, what do you tend to do?

❏ I get frustrated and stew.

❏ I talk to people who are smarter than I am.

❏ I pray for God to make the decision for me and give me a huge sign.

❏ I pray for wisdom.

What do you need to change in order to experience wisdom the way Solomon and Daniel did?

Humble Circumstances

As you read the next four passages, write down what God's people are to focus on.

MATTHEW 23:11-12   *1 TIMOTHY 6:7-11*

PHILIPPIANS 4:11-13   *HEBREWS 13:5-6*

When you think about your potential career path, what questions do you consider?

❏ How much money will I make?

❏ What kind of status will I have?

❏ How happy will I be?

❏ What is God calling me to do?

What changes do you need to make in order to pursue the things of God (which may lead to humble circumstances) rather than the things of the world (which may lead to comfortable—or even luxurious—circumstances)?

Temptation

As you read the following passages, look for the answers to these questions:

— What's the root of temptation?

— What are the consequences of caving in to temptation?

— What can give you strength to beat temptation?

GENESIS 3:1-7

_____

_____

_____

2 CORINTHIANS 12:7-10

_____

_____

_____

HEBREWS 2:17-3:1

_____

_____

JAMES 1:13-15

_____

_____

When you're tempted, what do you tend to do?

❒ Cave

❒ Resist for awhile, then rationalize a cave-in

❒ Flee from the temptation

Write down three observations from these verses—things to do or ways to think—that can help you beat temptation in your life.

_____

_____

KEEP IT SIMPLE
James 1:19-27

God has always been generous with people who are obedient. From Day One (actually from Da_y Six, beginning with the debut of man), God has placed a premium on obedience. We're all required to know God's commands, but heeding them seems to come with a special set of promises. As you prepare to study James again, read Deuteronomy 6:1-3. These are the words of Moses, spoken as he prepared God's people to take possession of the Promised Land. Notice the emphasis on heeding God's decrees and the payoff for doing so.

These are the commands, decrees and laws the Lord your God directed me to teach you to observe in the land that you are crossing the Jordan to possess, so that you, your children and their children after them may fear the Lord your God as long as you live by keeping all his decrees and commands that I give you, and so that you may enjoy long life. Hear, O Israel, and be careful to obey so that it may go well with you and that you may increase greatly in a land flowing with milk and honey, just as the Lord, the God of your fathers, promised you.

—Deuteronomy 6:1-3

SEARCH

Read instructions before engaging life

Read The Letter—James 1:19-27. As you read, mark every instruction James gives his readers. Look back at what you marked and list the instructions in this passage.

_____

_____

Read the passage a second time and jot down everything you learn about God.

_____

REFLECTION

Finally, a reason to stop praying (about one thing, at least)

How many times have you asked God about his will for your life? Have you ever realized God has already told you what his will is? In just these nine verses, we are given guidelines concerning our inner and outer behavior—behavior that God desires and accepts. Perhaps doing God's will is simpler than we think.

For the next few minutes, think about a 60-day stretch in your life—the past 30 days and the next 30 days. Rate yourself on how well you've obeyed each of these instructions over the past 30 days. If God's Spirit brings to mind specific situations when you blew it, write them down.

INSTRUCTIONS	PAST 30 DAYS	NEXT 30 DAYS
BE QUICK TO LISTEN, SLOW TO SPEAK (1:19)		
BE SLOW TO BECOME ANGRY (1:19)		
GET RID OF ALL MORAL FILTH AND EVIL (1:21)		
HUMBLY ACCEPT THE WORD PLANTED IN YOU (1:21)		
DO WHAT THE WORD SAYS (1:22)		
KEEP A TIGHT REIN ON YOUR TONGUE (1:26)		
LOOK AFTER ORPHANS AND WIDOWS IN DISTRESS (1:27)		
KEEP FROM BEING POLLUTED BY THE WORLD (1:27)		

Now for the challenge. What can you do over the next 30 days to better obey these instructions? Try to respond with specific examples. For instance, next to the instruction to look after widows and orphans, write down specific names, along with tasks you can do in the coming month. (For example, rake Mrs. Adam's leaves.)

We're given a promise in James 1:25—something we're guaranteed if we follow the perfect law. Write that promise in the space below.

CROSS-REFERENCES

Hear, then do

James 1:25 emphasizes a pattern that shows up throughout the entire Bible—first hear, then do the Word. It's also a pattern that figures prominently in Jesus' teaching. If the tight relationship between hearing and doing hasn't sunk in yet (or even if it has), read the words of Jesus in each of the following verses. Be sure to note the context of each passage. Then write down the phrases Jesus uses for hearing and doing, along with any promises you can enjoy when you hear and do the Word of God.

LUKE 11:28

JOHN 14:21

_____

_____

MATTHEW 7:24-25

_____

_____

SEARCH
The deceit factor

James warns us of two ways in which we can deceive ourselves. Find these warnings in James 1:19-27 and write them here.

_____

_____

Could you be deceived in these areas? The problem with self-deception is that if we're deceiving ourselves, we may not even know it! Take a couple of minutes to assess your self-deception level by prayerfully responding to the following questions.

Warning 1: Don't merely listen to the Word; do what it says.

Think about your activities over the past 10 days. Is your agenda the same as God's? If not, whose agenda have you been doing—yours or God's?

_____

_____

How often does your personal Bible study lead to action—a significant response to your study?

_____

_____

Think about the last time you were motivated or challenged by a Christian speaker or teacher. About how long ago was that? What actions resulted from that motivation once you got home?

_____

Consider the prevalence of Christian television, music, magazines, books, and conferences today—and the number of believers who "hear the Word" through these media. Is the gospel penetrating our culture as a result of all the church is hearing? Compare what you see in the church at large to what you read in James 1:22-25.

_____

_____

Warning 2: Keep a tight rein on your tongue.

The phrase "tight rein" probably relates to James' earlier reference to being slow to speak (1:19). We'll be looking at the devastating effects of gossip later in our study of James.

Picture the last time someone complained to you about something you did, such as a decision you made or a plan you implemented. Were you slow to speak and quick to listen?

_____

_____

When you're in a position to defend your opinion, can you describe yourself as having a tight rein on your tongue? Does the need to win override the Bible's command to control what you say?

_____

_____

APPLICATION
So act already!

Wherever God has spoken to your heart—impressed an idea into your mind—is where you need to apply what you've uncovered in James 1. If you need some suggestions for doing the instructions from this section of James, read over the Apply exercise in Teach It. Then take some action! Perhaps you need to pick up the phone and call a dear widow you know. Maybe you need to apologize to someone for being quick to speak and slow to listen.

But here's a word of warning: Don't do the Word simply to set an example for your students. That's noble, but it's not authentic. Do the Word out of obedience to what God has put on your heart. In fact, don't finish this study time until God's Spirit has led you to a specific action. Then do it!

Be sure to read Teach It so that you're familiar with the flow of the session—particularly the Application and Closing exercises.

KEEP IT SIMPLE
James 1:19-27

■ OPENING

Brainstorm ways to help students think about God's will for their lives.

■ SEARCH

Read instructions before engaging life
Students will consider what James means by the righteous life.

■ REFLECTION

From the inside out
Students will process key instructions James gives regarding internal and external behavior.

■ SOLITUDE

Hear, then do
This exercise examines Bible verses in which Jesus emphasizes the same principles that James gives.

■ APPLICATION

So act already!
Students will identify steps they can take to apply the teachings covered in James 1:19-27.

■ CLOSING

Start simple
Commission students who plan to implement one of the ministries introduced in this chapter.

YOU'LL NEED

a whiteboard and markers

Bibles

pens

copies of Keep It Simple (pages 39-40), one for each student

copies of The Letter—James 1 (page 146), one for each new student

colored pencils

Students who were present for the last session should use the copies of James 1 they have already marked.

OPENING

After the group has gathered, distribute materials and open the session with prayer. Let your kids report on how they've been doing on their applications. Remind the students that God has something specific he wants to say to each person in this study of James. Then ask questions along this line:

▸ *Is there anything we can pray for that would help you focus on what God wants to say to you today? Are there distractions Satan is using—busyness, drowsiness, general stress—that we need to pray about?*

Allow the students to share briefly. Then pray that the Word can cut through the distractions for maximum impact on their lives.

After prayer, get the conversation rolling with a few questions.

> ▸ *What are some ways people can know God's will?*

> ▸ *As you've moved into your high school years, have you begun asking questions about knowing God's will for your life?*

> ▸ *How do you discover God's will for your life?*

Transition into the next exercise by saying something like—

> ▸ *By the time we finish this session, we may find that discovering God's will is easier than we think.*

Read instructions before engaging life

Draw your students' attention to The Letter—James 1.

> ▸ *James often indicates a change in subject with the phrase "my brothers." So what might we conclude about James 1:19?*
> ▸ *Read The Letter—James 1:19-27. As you read, draw a cloud over every reference to God and underline every reference that relates to the readers of the letter.*

While the students are reading, draw the framework for the following two-column chart on the board. This is what it will look like when finished:

INSTRUCTIONS	PAST 30 DAYS	NEXT 30 DAYS
BE QUICK TO LISTEN, SLOW TO SPEAK (1:19)		
BE SLOW TO BECOME ANGRY (1:19)		
GET RID OF ALL MORAL FILTH AND EVIL (1:21)		
HUMBLY ACCEPT THE WORD PLANTED IN YOU (1:21)		
DO WHAT THE WORD SAYS (1:22)		
KEEP A TIGHT REIN ON YOUR TONGUE (1:26)		
LOOK AFTER ORPHANS AND WIDOWS IN DISTRESS (1:27)		
KEEP FROM BEING POLLUTED BY THE WORLD (1:27)		

After a few minutes, ask the group members to look back at the clouds they marked.

▸ *What do you learn about God in this passage?*

He desires that we live a righteous life (1:20).

God wants us to look after orphans and widows and keep ourselves from being polluted by the world—"pure and faultless religion" (1:27).

▸ *Look back at the verses you marked about James' readers. What commands or instructions does James give his audience? As we list these on the board, we'll begin to see a picture of the righteous life James is referring to.*

List their responses in the second column, one instruction per line. Ask the students to write the same information on their handouts.

REFLECTION

From the inside out

▸ *These instructions can be classified in two categories: our inner life and our outer life. Which of these instructions are inner and which are outer?*

Inner

Be slow to become angry (1:19)

Get rid of all moral filth and evil (1:21)

Humbly accept the Word planted in you (1:21)

Keep yourself from being polluted by the world (1:27)

Outer

Be quick to listen, slow to speak (1:19)

Do what the Word says (1:22)

Keep a tight rein on your tongue (1:26)

Look after orphans and widows in distress (1:27)

Have a volunteer come to the board and circle the inner-related instructions and draw a box around the outer-related instructions. You may come to some different conclusions about which category some instructions fit into.

▸ *How can we—as a group or as individuals—start obeying these instructions or obey them more consistently? Give me two or three ideas for each instruction.*

Encourage the students to be specific and practical. For example, when you get to the widows and orphans in 1:27, write down names of specific people the group can help. Write their ideas in the third column on the whiteboard and students can write them on their handout.

▸ *What did James say will happen if we do these things?*

We will be blessed in what we do (1:25).

Leave the ideas on the board. You'll be referring to them later in the session.

Hear, then do

▸ *God has always put a premium on doing his commands, which is why James could promise that we'll be blessed when we obey God's Word. We're going to spend some time in solitude now, studying what Jesus had to say on this subject.*

▸ *Take your Bibles and handouts to a place where you can have a little privacy with God. Follow the instructions on your handout for the Solitude exercise and interact with God through prayer about the connection between hearing his Word and doing his Word.*

After about 10 minutes, call the group back together.

▸ *In the passages you just read, what two-step process does Jesus apply to his words and commands?*

▸ *How have you been doing with these two steps lately?*

We need to know his commands and obey them.

Ask volunteers to share where they rated themselves on the scales and what their rationale is.

▸ *Jesus attaches some hefty promises to these two steps—a good indicator that they're crucial for Christians. What adjustments do you need to make in your life in order to experience these promises?*

So act already!

Granted, you and your group members are busy. The whole world is busy! But could it be that God is waiting for us to take James 1:22 more seriously? Spend the next few minutes strategizing ways you and your students can listen to the Word and put into practice the instructions they've uncovered in James 1. Listed below are some examples to help the group get out of the starting block.

▸ *We're going to close with a group work session to help each of us crank up the intensity for hearing and doing the Word. What are some practical steps we can take to hear the Word better? What are some things we can do to put the Word into practice?*

As the group discusses the action steps they can take, have them jot down notes on the chart near the end of their handouts. You might suggest that they expand on the ideas listed on the board in the column. Here are some suggestions:

Hear the Word

— Spend the next 30 days reading one of the four gospels—Matthew, Mark, Luke, or John. Keep a journal of everything Jesus commanded and taught. As you read each parable, write down the main point Jesus is making.

— Immerse yourself in an entire book of the Bible. Start small, say a one-chapter book like 2 John or 3 John. Make that book a part of your life for the next few weeks. Look for things like warnings, instructions, and info about God, Jesus, and the Holy Spirit. Become your family's authority on one of these books. Then move to a book like Titus (three chapters).

Do the Word

— Have a church directory or phone book handy. If you listed specific names on the whiteboard earlier, divvy up the names and phone numbers of these people. Have one or two students make a phone call, drop in for a visit, or volunteer to help with some chores.

Check with your county's children's services department; perhaps you can provide a group birthday party, Christmas party, or game night at a children's home.

— Take a 10-day fast from "the things of the world." Your students will know what has the potential to pollute them—what they read, watch, listen to, or talk about. Ask them to write two or three things to avoid on their Do the Word list.

CLOSING

Start simple

Take your teens back to the discussion at the beginning of the session.

▸ *Did today's Scriptures make it easier to know God's will for your life? If so, in what ways?*

Steer the discussion to the following conclusion:

When we do what God reveals in his Word, we're doing his will. When we look after widows and orphans in their distress and keep from being polluted by the world, we're doing what God accepts as "pure and faultless"—his will.

▸ *So if you want to discover God's will for your life, based on James, how would you get started?*

Let the group discuss this one for a minute. Wrap up with thoughts like this:

▸ *Obeying God in the simple things is a great starting point for obeying him in the bigger areas of life. For example, as you help out a widow in your neighborhood, God may see he can trust you with something else. He may move you on to another ministry that defines your life's calling, or he may simply bring more orphans and widows your way. By faithfully obeying God, you'll soon discover that you're doing his will for your life—and you'll be blessed in all you do.*

Before closing in prayer, ask whether anyone would like to take God up on his idea of pursuing "pure and faultless religion"—ministry to widows or orphans. If so, pray a prayer of dedication for those who wish to pursue this type of ministry.

KEEP IT SIMPLE
James 1:19-27

SEARCH

Read instructions before engaging life

Read James 1:19-27, drawing a cloud over every reference to God and underlining every reference that relates to the readers of the letter. In the first column list the instructions or commands given by James.

As your group brainstorms specific ways to respond to each instruction, list the ideas in the second column.

We'll come back to the third and fourth columns later.

READ INSTRUCTIONS BEFORE ENGAGING LIFE

INSTRUCTIONS	STARTING NOW!	LAST 30 DAYS	NEXT 30 DAYS

SOLITUDE

Hear, then do

Read the Bible verses in the first column. As you read, look for the answers to the questions in the second and third columns. Write them down.

HEAR, THEN DO

BIBLE PASSAGE	WHAT ARE WE TO DO?	WHAT'S THE PROMISE?
LUKE 11:28		
MATTHEW 7:24–25		
JOHN 14:21		

What's the two-step process in each of these passages?

Step 1   **Step 2**

How are you doing with these two steps? Rate yourself on the scales below.

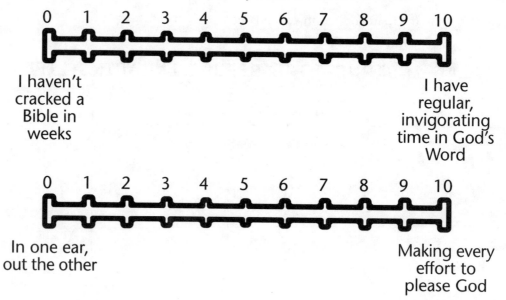

0 1 2 3 4 5 6 7 8 9 10

I haven't cracked a Bible in weeks   I have regular, invigorating time in God's Word

0 1 2 3 4 5 6 7 8 9 10

In one ear, out the other   Making every effort to please God

Think for a minute about a 60-day stretch in your life—the past 30 days and the next 30 days. You'll notice two columns with these headings in the first chart on this handout. Evaluate how well you've obeyed each instruction over the past 30 days. Indicate your response by putting a plus sign or a minus sign beside each instruction in the third column. In the fourth column, write a specific way you could do each instruction over the next month. Then put these words into practice!

APPLICATION

So act already!

As the group develops some practical steps to hear and do the Word more effectively, jot down the ideas:

Hear the Word   Do the Word

_____

_____

_____

NOTHIN' BUT HEART
James 2:1-13

SESSION
4

NOTHIN'
BUT
HEART

JAMES
2:1-13

Congratulations! As you finish today's session preparation, you're one-fourth of the way through this study in James. In the last three weeks as you've thoroughly studied the first chapter of James' letter, it's quite possible you've been spending more time than usual in God's Word. As you've studied, have you noticed an elevated desire to know and obey God? The real purpose of an in-depth Bible study isn't simply to know more about the book but to know God himself. As we know God, our desire to obey him—follow him wholeheartedly—naturally increases.

You've probably noticed that James doesn't leave much room for guesswork on ways to obey God. As you prepare for today's study in James 2, take a moment to hear what the apostle Peter—a man who knew a lot about obedience—has to say about letting the Word change your behavior.

Now that you have purified yourselves by obeying the truth so that you have sincere love for your brothers, love one another deeply, from the heart. For you have been born again, not of perishable seed, but of imperishable, through the living and enduring word of God. For, "All men are like grass, and all their glory is like the flowers of the field; the grass withers and the flowers fall, but the word of the Lord stands forever." And this is the word that was preached to you.
—1 Peter 1:22-25

SEARCH

Favoritism 101

Read The Letter—James 2:1-13. As you read, mark each of the following with a unique symbol or color:

— References to favoritism, the poor, and the rich

— References to the readers of James' letter

— References to God

Take a moment to process what you've read by answering the following questions (classic who, what, when, where, why, and how questions).

What instructions does James give his readers?

_____

_____

What do you learn about favoritism?

_____

_____

What do you learn about God?

_____

_____

What conclusions can you draw about the situation of the recipients of James' letter?

_____

_____

How are they described?

_____

_____

What's been done to them?

_____

_____

What have they been doing that runs counter to God's desires?

_____

_____

How are they like you?

_____

_____

How are they like the students in your ministry?

_____

_____

CROSS-REFERENCES

The poor—near and dear to God's heart

The message of the gospel is the great socioeconomic equalizer. The external stuff—clothes, salary, house, car—really doesn't matter. God sees nothing but the heart when he's dishing out grace and mercy. When we're carrying out the ministry of the gospel, he asks us to look at the same thing. Our tendency, however, is to focus on the externals and gravitate toward those who are most like us—which is the first step in showing favoritism.

The significance of this next exercise is huge. To guarantee that you don't rush it, grab a glass of your favorite beverage and spend some time letting the Lord speak to your heart about one of his favorite subjects: the poor. As you read each of the following passages, jot down anything you learn about ministering to the poor.

What God says about the subject

Leviticus 19:15

_____

_____

Zechariah 7:8-12

_____

Deuteronomy 15:7-11

_____

_____

SESSION
4
NOTHIN'
BUT
HEART

JAMES
2:1-13

What Jesus says about the subject

Luke 4:18-19

_____

_____

Luke 14:12-14

_____

_____

Luke 12:29-34

_____

_____

What the first Christians say about the subject

Acts 10:1-2

_____

_____

Acts 24:17

_____

_____

Romans 15:25-26

_____

_____

Galatians 2:9-10

_____

_____

What you say about the subject

_____

_____

What conclusions are you coming to concerning the priority of ministering to the poor?

_____

_____

How do your priorities compare with God's priorities?

_____

Of course you don't discriminate...or do you?

Consider the following paraphrase of James 2:2-4.

You're hosting an outreach event in order to launch an evangelism effort at the local high school. Through the door walks a student who's the son of a prominent family in your community and a favorite among the faculty and students at the school. Behind him is a teen who's introverted and quiet. This student is actually disliked at the school because he's unmotivated and disrespectful. If you make every effort to establish a relationship with the first student and hope that your volunteers make contact with the second student, haven't you discriminated among your students and become a judge with evil thoughts?

Well? Have you? Take a moment to reflect on any situations in which you operated with even a hint of the discrimination James describes. In the space below, write what comes to mind.

_____

_____

Think about the poor who are involved in your student ministry. (You may need to broaden your definition of the poor to include those who are poor in social skills, leadership abilities, intellect, athletic abilities, or interpersonal relationships.) Have you ever, even momentarily, looked at such a student and thought, "This isn't somebody I can build a program around"?

_____

_____

If you spend time on a school campus connecting with students, consider that setting for a moment. With whom do you seek to build relationships? Is it with students in leadership? Popular kids? Athletes?

_____

_____

What is God saying to you about the poor around you?

_____

_____

What is he prompting you to do regarding the poor in your student ministry?

_____

_____

Be sure to read Teach It so you're familiar with the flow of the group session. One exercise includes a discussion of steps your students can take to accept and affirm anyone who comes in contact with your group's ministry—rich or poor. You'll want to give some thought to this exercise before the group meets.

NOTHIN' BUT HEART
James 2:1-13

SESSION
4
NOTHIN'
BUT
HEART

JAMES
2:1-13

■OPENING

After the group has gathered, distribute materials and open the session with prayer. Begin with a fun discussion about student favorites.

■SEARCH

Favoritism 101
Students will discover some incisive instructions from James regarding favoritism.

■REFLECTION

Of course you don't discriminate...or do you?
This group discussion will allow students to compare James' instructions on favoritism with what's happening in their group.

■SOLITUDE

The poor—near and dear to God's heart
Students will explore other Bible passages that instruct believers to care for the poor.

■REFLECTION

The futility of favoritism
Students will work as a group to process what God impressed upon them during Solitude.

■APPLICATION

Thus saith the Lord: "No cliques!"
Students will take practical steps to minimize playing favorites—as individuals and as a group.

■CLOSING

Prayer of forgiveness

YOU'LL NEED
a whiteboard and markers
Bibles
pens
copies of Nothin' but Heart (pages 49-50), one for each student
copies of The Letter—James 2 (page 147), one for each student
colored pencils

OPENING

Gather your teens together, distribute materials, and open the session with prayer. Check in with group members on their applications. Then jump into the session with these questions:

▸ *What's your favorite current TV show?*

▸ *What's your favorite old show (in reruns or off the air)?*

▸ *What's your favorite binge food?*

▸ *Who's your favorite person in this group?*

The last question may catch them off guard. Whether you have them answer it or not, use the question to segue into the subject of the session.

▸ *When is it good to have favorites and when is it bad?*

Favoritism 101

▸ *James hits the subject of playing favorites directly in James 2. Read The Letter—James 2:1-13. Use colors to mark every mention of favoritism, the poor, and the rich. Use another color to mark every reference to the readers of James' letter. Look for the key word* you. *Use another color to mark every mention of God.*

Ask the students to suggest symbols they could use to mark references to the poor, the rich, James' audience, and God. The plan may be as simple as underlining references to favoritism, circling references to James' readers, and drawing a cloud for God.

After about five minutes ask the students to look back at what they marked.

▸ *What instructions to the readers do you see?*

Don't show favoritism (2:1).

Speak and act as those who are going to be judged by the law that gives freedom (2:12).

▸ *What did you learn about favoritism?*

We sin if we show favoritism (2:9).

▸ *What did you learn about God?*

He has chosen the poor to be rich in faith and to inherit the kingdom (2:5).

He has promised the kingdom to those who love him (2:5).

▸ *What conclusions can you draw about what's going on among James' readers?*

They've insulted the poor (2:6).

They must be overlooking the poor and catering to the rich and influential—the very people who are apparently exploiting them.

▸ *James makes some strong statements about favoritism. Out of all these verses, which ones pack the most punch in motivating his readers—us included—to stop playing favorites?*

Let the discussion be open-ended but see if you can guide your group to can agree on these two statements:

"As believers in our glorious Lord Jesus Christ, don't show favoritism" (2:1).

"But if you show favoritism, you sin" (2:9).

SESSION

4

NOTHIN'
BUT
HEART

JAMES
2:1-13

REFLECTION

Of course you don't discriminate...or do you?

> ‣ *In our ministry, how are we showing favoritism?*

Let students discuss the question for a couple of minutes before saying:

> ‣ *If James were writing this letter with our group in mind, how might he have worded verses 2-4? Take a minute to paraphrase these verses, using examples from our group. For example, instead of saying, "a man wearing fine clothes," you might say, "a senior everybody likes."*

After a few minutes ask for volunteers to share their versions of James 2:2-4.

> ‣ *For us, who might "the poor man in shabby clothes" be?*

If the students already mentioned examples as they read their versions of James 2:2-4, list these on the whiteboard. Brainstorm other poor-man examples and add them to the list.

SOLITUDE

The poor—near and dear to God's heart

> ‣ *The subject of the poor is addressed in nearly every book of the Bible. For the next few minutes, we're going to look at a few of these passages during a personal retreat with God's Word. Keep in mind the examples we just discussed as you read about the poor in these passages.*

Ask the students to find some personal space, taking their Bibles and handouts.

REFLECTION

The futility of favoritism

After about 15 minutes, call the kids back together and discuss questions like these:

> ‣ *What insights or conclusions did you come up with regarding ministering to the poor?*

> ‣ *Have you personally been guilty of showing favoritism? Without naming names, give us an idea of when you've shown favoritism.*

▶ *How have we as a group been guilty of showing favoritism? How should we describe our actions? What's the appropriate response to correct our course?*

Point out that it would be easy to dismiss favoritism as a minor oversight (corrected by trying not to do it again) or a mistake (corrected by apologizing and rectifying the mistake). But James calls it a sin (James 2:9), which means it can only be corrected through repentance and forgiveness.

APPLICATION

Thus saith the Lord: "No cliques!"

▶ *As a group, what steps do we need to take to repent of the favoritism we've shown?*

▶ *What are some ongoing steps we can take to not only avoid favoritism but also to affirm everyone who has contact with our student ministry?*

It's extremely important to avoid appearing arrogant or superior. Be tactful as you initiate contact and offer assistance.

Here are some suggestions:

— Identify a "poor" church or student ministry in your community that could benefit from your support. (Remember "poor" isn't limited to finances.) Work with them to develop a way of supporting the ministry, perhaps by—

    a. raising funds

    b. tithing 10 percent of your group's regular fundraising efforts

    c. giving time or other resources to enable them to offer an event or pursue a project

— Implement a follow-up program for all first-time guests. The program might include home visits, personal invitations to activities, free Bibles, CDs or candy bars, or other innovative ideas.

— Train students to be aware of others who are quiet, introverted, or alone. Help them develop skills to initiate conversations, to be inclusive, and to introduce kids to new friends.

— Teens who are blessed with leadership skills, extroverted personalities, and enthusiasm can form a team dedicated to helping newcomers and guests be accepted and integrated into the larger group.

Remind your group members that none of these activities are for the sake of the group or ministry; they're for the sake of the gospel.

CLOSING

Prayer of forgiveness

Encourage students to continue thinking of ways in which they—individually or as a group—have shown favoritism. Challenge them to repent of their sins and ask forgiveness from those they've slighted.

End the session with prayer.

Next week your teens will be asked to refer to their sheets from previous sessions. Remind them to bring their notebooks or folders.

NOTHIN' BUT HEART
James 2:1-13

SESSION
4
NOTHIN'
BUT
HEART

JAMES
2:1-13

REFLECTION

Of course you don't discriminate...or do you?

Paraphrase James 2:2-4.

_____

_____

SOLITUDE

The poor—near and dear to God's heart

As you read the following passages, write down everything you learn—using as much detail as possible—about ministering to the poor.

What God says about the subject

LEVITICUS 19:15   *ZECHARIAH 7:8-12*

_____   _____

DEUTERONOMY 15:7-11

_____

What Jesus says about the subject

LUKE 4:18-19   *LUKE 12:29-34*

_____   _____

LUKE 14:12-14

_____

What the first Christians say about the subject

ACTS 10:1-2

_____

_____

ACTS 24:17

_____

_____

ROMANS 15:25-26

_____

_____

_____

GALATIANS 2:9-10

_____

_____

_____

What you say about the subject

What conclusions are you coming to concerning the priority of ministering to the poor?

_____

_____

How do your priorities compare with God's priorities?

_____

_____

FAITH YOU CAN SEE
James 2:14-26

SESSION
5

FAITH
YOU CAN
SEE

JAMES
2:14-26

In an intimate conversation with his closest friends, Jesus makes an outlandish promise. Read his words below and note what the Lord says will happen if his disciples followed through on a few key actions.

Whoever has my commands and obeys them, he is the one who loves me. He who loves me will be loved by my Father, and I too will love him and show myself to him.

—John 14:21

Let's get this straight. In the passage above, underline the two things we can do to show our love for Jesus. Then circle three things we'll enjoy when we *have* and *obey* Jesus' commands. Did you catch the third one—that Jesus will *show himself* to us? When was the last time Jesus really showed himself to you? Don't explain away that verse, thinking that Jesus is talking about his second coming—the day when he'll show himself to all the earth. He's talking about here and now, and it sounds like a fairly conspicuous manifestation!

Though written by James in terms of its human authorship, the book of James was authored by the Holy Spirit. Therefore it contains the words and commands of Jesus, whether Jesus literally spoke them or not. So let's give Jesus' promise in John 14 a try. Make today's session preparation a time dedicated to *having* Jesus' Word. Let's commit to *obeying* whatever he impresses onto our hearts, even if it's the subtlest impression.

Then look for an outpouring of love from Jesus and the Father. And expect the outlandish…a personal revelation of Jesus to you! It's a great promise—but don't neglect your part of the bargain.

REVIEW

Track the themes

Take a few minutes to review what you've seen in James so far. Notice what you've marked on your copy of The Letter. Do you begin to get a sense of why James wrote this letter? What themes are emerging?

It's a straight line from faith to deeds

You may have noted that throughout his epistle, James resolves nearly every dilemma by calling for tangible, visible behavior from his readers—actions that can be seen—doing what the Word says, looking after widows and orphans, and refraining from favoritism.

Read The Letter—James 2:14-26. Use your colored pencils to uniquely mark the words *faith* and *deeds* (including synonyms like *works* and *action*).

After you've read and marked the passage, look back at the verses that mention both faith and deeds/works/action. List below everything James says about the relationship between the two.

_____

_____

In your own words, what's the connection between faith and deeds?

_____

_____

Faith versus works—or faith and works?

Faith versus works constitutes one of the great debates of the Christian age. After reading James 2, people often ask questions like these: Isn't salvation a free gift, dependent on our faith, not works? What about Romans 5:1: "Since we have been justified through faith, we have peace with God through our Lord Jesus Christ"?

Let's sort it out.

Paul says—

> *Therefore, since we have been justified through faith, we have peace with God through our Lord Jesus Christ.*
>
> —Romans 5:1

> *For it is by grace you have been saved, through faith—and this not from yourselves, it is the gift of God—not by works, so that no one can boast.*
>
> —Ephesians 2:8-9

James says—

> *You see that a person is justified by what he does and not by faith alone.*
>
> —James 2:24

At a glance, Paul and James seem to contradict one another. The great reformer Martin Luther thought that because of this apparent contradiction, the book of James should have been removed from the canon of Scripture. (He made such statements in the preface of an early edition of the Luther Bible but removed them in later editions.)

The irony is that both Paul and Luther were experiencing similar circumstances. In Paul's day the people—Jews and deceived Gentiles—were using works of the law for salvation. In Luther's day it was the works of the church that the people relied on. In both cases these works were not the same deeds spoken of by James.

Throughout the New Testament, when Paul refers to works he means works of the law—works that the Jews and legalistic Gentiles performed in order to achieve salvation. When James speaks of works, he means deeds done as a result of salvation.

You can categorize the two types of works this way: works done before salvation, which are useless in terms of securing salvation, and works done after salvation, which are useful in that they please God and fulfill the mission of Christ.

SESSION
5

FAITH
YOU CAN
SEE

JAMES
2:14-26

CROSS-REFERENCES
Define the deeds

The passages below give a more complete picture of the relationship between faith and deeds. Read these from your Bible, carefully observing the context of each passage. Then record in the columns anything you learn about the works or deeds mentioned. (The New International Version often uses the phrase "observing the law".)

DEFINE THE DEEDS

BIBLE VERSES	DEEDS WE'RE TO DO	CAUTIONS ABOUT OUR DEEDS
MATTHEW 25:31-46		
JOHN 3:21		
ROMANS 3:20-28		
GALATIANS 2:15-16		
GALATIANS 5:6		
EPHESIANS 2:8-10 (NOTE VERSE 10)		
TITUS 3:8		

Circle anything you recorded in the previous chart that parallels James' take on deeds in James 2. Based on your study so far, what kinds of deeds are we asked to do?

_____

_____

In your own words, write the definitive conclusion James makes about the connection between faith and actions in James 2:22.

_____

_____

REFLECTION

How are the vital signs of your faith?

You might say that Paul and James address two extremes of a single perspective. Paul was speaking to new believers who felt compelled to observe the law to achieve or maintain a saving relationship with God. James is encouraging established believers to see that true faith leads to action. After all, if faith doesn't result in action, can you really call it faith? People can say that they believe in the principles of aerodynamics, but if they're unwilling to fly in a plane, what good is their belief? By the same token, they can talk about their faith in the gospel, but if their actions don't back it up, how deep is that belief?

Every one of us is capable of living at either extreme. We can think our good works save us—or we can blow them off as unimportant in comparison to our faith in Christ. Take a minute or two to reflect on your own faith in Jesus.

Since faith without action is dead, what's the medical condition of your faith? Base your answer solely on your actions.

❏ dead   ❏ showing symptoms of sickness

❏ on life support   ❏ vital signs are improving

❏ in intensive care   ❏ alive and kickin'

❏ in the emergency room

Here's a tough question, one you may be tempted to skip—but don't. If your faith in Jesus Christ is not leading to action, could it be that you really...don't...believe? Deal with this question honestly before continuing. Write your thoughts.

_____

_____

_____

APPLICATION

Do good, and do it secretly

James uses three examples to illustrate the kinds of deeds he is talking about in chapter 2. Write them down in the first column. Think about the first item you've written down. What general type of deed is this or what is a key characteristic of it? Write that in the second column. Answer the same question for James' other examples. Then give examples of what we might do today that is similar to the biblical examples. Write those in the third column.

SESSION
5

FAITH
YOU CAN
SEE

JAMES
2:14-26

MODELS OF ACTION

JAMES' ILLUSTRATIONS	TYPES OR CHARACTERISTICS	CORRESPONDING DEEDS TODAY

If you need to refresh your memory about Rahab, read Joshua 2.

James' illustrations give us a great jump start on backing our faith with action; we don't have to search for ideas. We have no excuse for not locking on to a practical task that can put action to your faith: Do something about the physical needs of a brother or sister in Christ before the session with your students. Do it in secret—and keep it a secret!

Be sure to read Teach It so you're familiar with each exercise and the flow of the session. Ask the Lord to prepare the hearts of your students to hear and obey the spiritual truths they'll be uncovering in James 2.

FAITH YOU CAN SEE
James 2:14-26

SESSION

5

FAITH
YOU CAN
SEE

JAMES
2:14-26

■INTRO

Track the themes

After the group has gathered, distribute materials and open the session with prayer. Review what the group has studied so far to discover themes.

■SEARCH

It's a straight line from faith to deeds

Students will analyze the relationship between faith and action.

■SOLITUDE

Define the deeds

This exercise will help students gain a deeper understanding of the relationship between faith and good deeds.

■REFLECTION

How are the vital signs of your faith?

Students will evaluate how their deeds compare to the standards revealed in the Bible.

■APPLICATION

Do good and do it secretly

Through a group discussion of James' illustrations students will figure out ways to apply the truths in James 2.

■CLOSING

Needs and deeds

Students will be challenged to commit themselves to take action as a result of their study of James 2.

YOU'LL NEED

a whiteboard and markers

Bibles

pens

The Letter and handouts from Sessions 1-4

copies of Faith You Can See (pages 63-64), one for each student

copies of The Letter—James 2 (page 147), one for each new student

colored pencils

Your students will be asked to refer to their sheets from previous sessions. Some groups may need a reminder in advance to bring their notebooks or folders.

INTRO

Track the themes

Once the group has gathered, distribute materials and open the session with prayer.

▶ *Take a minute to look back over The Letter and handouts for James 1 and 2. What major themes have we seen in James so far?*

TEACH IT TEACH IT TEACH IT TEACH IT TEACH IT TEACH IT

As the students share their thoughts, elicit the observation that James is focused on practical action. In fact, he resolves almost every issue with an outward action his readers can do: persevere, be slow to become angry, do what the Word says, look after orphans and widows, don't play favorites, and so on.

It's a straight line from faith to deeds

Transition into the session with comments something like this:

> ▸ Obviously, James is encouraging his readers—including us—to respond to life's situations with godly action. The passage we're about to study puts a giant exclamation point on this encouragement.

> ▸ Read James 2:14-26 using The Letter. Use two different colors or symbols to mark the words faith and deeds. For example, circle faith and draw a box around deeds. When you mark the word deeds, include other words that mean the same thing, like works and action.

When most have finished reading and marking, continue with—

> ▸ Take a look at the verses that mention both faith and deeds. What does James say about the relationship between the two?

It does no good to have faith without deeds (2:14).

This kind of faith can't save you (2:14).

It does no good to wish people well but do nothing to help them physically (2:16).

Faith without action is dead (2:17).

Faith and action work together (2:22).

Faith is made complete by action (2:22).

You are justified by what you do and by faith (2:24).

List responses on the whiteboard. If any of the points are missing, you can suggest them yourself.

> ▸ How does James' teaching on the need for works square with the fact that salvation is a free gift?

> ▸ Do you agree or disagree with this statement: If you think you're a Christian but nothing in your life backs it up, then you're probably not a Christian. Explain your choice.

Define the deeds

> ▸ Since the beginning of Christianity, there's been a great debate about the value of works. Some think that because salvation is a free gift from God based on faith alone (we don't have to work for it), Christians don't have to do good works. Others think that good works are required for our salvation.

SESSION

5

FAITH
YOU CAN
SEE

JAMES
2:14-26

▶ *For the purpose of today's session, here's the bottom line: We do good works because we're Christians, not in order to become Christians.*

▶ *In a minute you're going to spend some time in solitude with God and the Bible, looking up some verses that will help you better understand the connection between faith and deeds. As you consider the passages and questions on your handout consider the very real possibility that God wants to take you to places you've never been before in your walk with him.*

Ask the students to take their Bibles, The Letter, and handouts to a place where they can get comfortable and be alone with God. Direct them to the Solitude section they should focus on. The instructions are on the handout.

APPLICATION

Do good and do it secretly

After about 15 minutes call the group back together. The finished chart on the student handout should look something like this

DEFINE THE DEEDS

BIBLE VERSES	DEEDS WE'RE TO DO	CAUTIONS ABOUT OUR DEEDS
MATTHEW 25:31-46		
JOHN 3:21	Be guided by truth; do what's right.	
ROMANS 3:20-28		Doing deeds alone won't make us right with God.
GALATIANS 2:15-16		
GALATIANS 5:6		
EPHESIANS 2:8-10		We aren't justified by observing the law (works).
TITUS 3:8	Do deeds driven by love.	

Since you aren't going to write ideas from this chart on the board as usual, check with your teens to see how they did filling in the chart. Let other students offer suggestions if anyone had difficulty.

▶ *What insights do you have now about the relationship between deeds and faith?*

There are deeds (deeds of the law) that don't save us and deeds that are an integral part of living out our faith, such as deeds of love (Galatians 5:6) and good works that are the result of a relationship with Christ (Ephesians 2:10; Titus 3:8).

Next you'll be talking with your students about James' illustrations of good deeds and what they might look like today. When you've finished the discussion, you should have a chart that's similar to this on your whiteboard.

DEEDS THEN AND NOW

JAMES' ILLUSTRATIONS	TYPES OR CHARACTERISTICS	CORRESPONDING DEEDS TODAY
Helping brothers and sisters with physical needs (2:15-16)	Meeting physical needs of people	Collect food for the church's food pantry; clean out closets and give away possessions.
Abraham sacrificing his son (2:21-22)	Sacrificial works	Baby-sit younger siblings so parents can go out on a Saturday night; donate all my savings to the International 30-hour famine; sponsor a child through Compassion or a similar group.
Rahab helping the spies (2:25)	Showing kindness and helping others	Tutor at the inner city after-school center.

▸ *James uses three illustrations to show the kind of works he is talking about. Look at James 2:14-26 again. What examples does he give?*

Make three columns on the board and write the illustrations in the first column as your kids mention them. Students can write the discussion information on their handouts.

▸ *What type of work does each illustration refer to or what is a main characteristic of it?*

Write the suggestions in the second column on the board.

▸ *What deeds can we do today to do the kind of works James is instructing us to do?*

You may want to give an example to get the ideas started. (See the completed chart at the beginning of this section.) Write the suggestions in the third column.

CLOSING

Needs and deeds

This segment of James is one of the most practical passages in the entire Bible. Don't close the session without giving students an opportunity to commit to some outward expression of faith. James gave several examples of outward action in the first two chapters of his letter.

▸ *Before we close, let's each lock in on something God may be calling us to do as a result of what we've studied in James 1 and 2. Maybe you can take an idea from the board—or take a minute to review The Letter and handouts we've worked on so far.*

SESSION

5

FAITH
YOU CAN
SEE

JAMES
2:14-26

After a few minutes let students share how they would like to respond. Lead the group in a brainstorming session about how they can encourage each other to follow through with their commitments. Here are two suggestions:

— Schedule a day (Saturday or a school holiday such as President's Day) when the group can meet for every meal. Between meals the students can do their acts of faith individually or as a group. Start early and make the last meal a late-night snack.

— Keep a giant Needs and Deeds list. Close this session by jotting on the list possible needs and good deeds that have emerged from the discussion. Over the next few weeks check off deeds as they're completed and add new needs as they arise. Ask a volunteer (or a set of volunteers) to manage this list.

Close with prayer.

FAITH YOU CAN SEE

James 2:14-26

SESSION
5
FAITH
YOU CAN
SEE

JAMES
2:14-26

SOLITUDE

Define the deeds

As you read these passages from your Bible, see what you can learn about works or deeds (the New International Version sometimes uses the phrase "observing the law"). You'll notice that while we're encouraged to do some deeds, we're cautioned about doing others. Record what you learn about each deed in the proper column.

DEFINE THE DEEDS

BIBLE VERSES	DEEDS WE'RE TO DO	CAUTIONS ABOUT OUR DEEDS
MATTHEW 25:31-46		
JOHN 3:21		
ROMANS 3:20-28		
GALATIANS 2:15-16		
GALATIANS 5:6		
EPHESIANS 2:8-10 (NOTE VERSE 10)		
TITUS 3:8		

Circle anything you wrote down that sounds similar to what James says about deeds.

Based on James and the passages in the chart, what should real faith look like?

What about you? Are faith and deeds working together in your life? This doesn't refer to church activities or personal devotions but to activities you do for others, the actions that give your faith arms and legs.

Since faith without action is dead, how would you classify the medical condition of your faith? (Base your answer solely on your actions—not your good intentions, your great personality, or your stellar leadership—just your actions!)

My faith is— ❏ dead ❏ on life support ❏ in intensive care

❏ in the emergency room ❏ showing symptoms of sickness ❏ vital signs are improving

❏ alive and kickin'

Think about the activities that have kept you busy over the past few months. Who have you been serving through these activities?

a. myself

b. my friends

c. those who can pay me back somehow

d. those who can't repay me, like the ones Jesus mentioned in Matthew 25

What's the Holy Spirit impressing upon you right now? Would you like your life to be geared more toward the actions James spoke of? Journal your thoughts.

_____

_____

You can start small—by showing those you live with that your faith means something. List some ways you can back up your faith with deeds when you're at home.

_____

_____

Now think a little bigger. How about fellow students at your church or school? How could you demonstrate your faith to them? Remember the old saying: "Actions speak louder than words."

_____

_____

APPLICATION

Do good and do it secretly

As your group discusses the illustrations James gives in chapter 2, you can write notes here.

DEEDS THEN AND NOW

JAMES' ILLUSTRATIONS	TYPES OR CHARACTERISTICS	CORRESPONDING DEEDS TODAY

FAITH YOU CAN SAY
James 3:1-12

SESSION
6

FAITH
YOU CAN
SAY

JAMES
3:1-12

Proverbs 2:1-5, a passage we read in Session 1, tells us we'll find the knowledge of God if we store up his commands inside us. Jesus, in dismissing an accusation from the Pharisees, gives another clue as to how our behavior will change when we store up the right stuff within us.

You brood of vipers, how can you who are evil say anything good? For out of the overflow of the heart the mouth speaks. The good man brings good things out of the good stored up in him, and the evil man brings evil things out of the evil stored up in him. But I tell you that men will have to give account on the day of judgment for every careless word they have spoken. For by your words you will be acquitted, and by your words you will be condemned.

—Matthew 12:34-37

As the Spirit softens your heart in today's study of God's Word, don't overlook one of the most fundamental applications for anything we learn from Scripture—the words we speak. As you'll see in James 3, if God's people could just master this problem area, the world would be a much better place.

SEARCH

What James wrote about tongues

Read The Letter—James 3:1-12. As you read, draw a tongue or lips over every mention of the tongue. Then look back at your markings and make a detailed list of everything James teaches concerning the tongue.

James uses three illustrations in verses 3-5 to make his point about the tongue. Each illustration consists of a small item connected to a large item. Record these in the space below.

Small items   Large items
_____   _____
_____   _____
_____   _____

Reread James 3:1-12. This time look for anything specific James' readers may have been doing to warrant such stern warnings about their tongues.

_____

Big damage done by fire, hurricanes—and tongues

Think for a minute about any recent situations in which you saw someone's tongue spark forest fire-sized damage. (Write in code if necessary.)

_____

_____

Have you ever been guilty of using your tongue in the same manner as James' readers—to curse men, who are made in God's image?

_____

_____

It's worth noting that James doesn't appear to be referring only to fellow believers. The word *men* implies people outside the church as well as brothers and sisters in Christ.

Consider this scenario: Have you ever observed the downfall of notorious unbelievers (such as philanderers, pornographers, unethical employers, deceptive politicians, and the like) and expressed that they're getting what they deserve? Note your thoughts.

_____

_____

You should have listed about seven observations in the first question of this lesson. Circle two items: the one you find the most insightful and the one that most convicts you. We'll come back to these in a moment.

A tongue questionnaire

As you read the following Bible verses, look for the answers to the questions in the chart. (The passages will not necessarily answer every question.)

A TONGUE QUESTIONNAIRE

SESSION
6

FAITH
YOU CAN
SAY

JAMES
3:1-12

BIBLE PASSAGES	HOW CAN THE TONGUE BE USED DESTRUCTIVELY?	HOW CAN THE TONGUE BE USED CONSTRUCTIVELY?	WHAT IS THE SOURCE OF WHAT THE MOUTH SPEAKS?
PROVERBS 16:28			
PROVERBS 17:9			
MATTHEW 12:33-37			
ROMANS 10:8-10			
EPHESIANS 4:29			
EPHESIANS 6:19-20			

APPLICATION

The power of your tongue

How does your tongue spend most of its time?

❒ Praising God

❒ Cursing man

❒ Declaring the mysteries of the gospel

If even one percent of your time is spent cursing man, James 3:9-12 speaks directly to your situation. Write down the examples James gave of things that don't mix.

In what areas of your speech do you struggle most?

❏ Lying

❏ Telling half-truths

❏ Presenting people, even friends, in a negative light

❏ Talking about others' struggles and mistakes

❏ Putting myself in a positive light at the expense of someone else

❏ Passing along insightful information about people to others

❏ Other (name it)

Earlier you were asked to circle two observations in your list about the tongue—one that you found most insightful, one that was most convicting. Take a moment to pray about these two truths, asking the Lord to give you wisdom about how to reflect the behavior he desires. (Remember what God promised concerning wisdom in James 1:5!)

What's your tongue going to be?

❏ An uplifting vessel that praises God, encourages others, and declares the message of the gospel.

❏ An unwholesome vessel that curses men and divides friends.

Commit yourself to doing the right thing. Consider what could happen in the church and in the world if God's people—starting with you and your student ministry—would obey these truths about the tongue.

Before you close your book be sure to read over Teach It so that you're familiar with the flow of the activities you'll be doing with your students.

FAITH YOU CAN SAY
James 3:1-12

SESSION

6

FAITH
YOU CAN
SAY

JAMES
3:1-12

■OPENING

Introduce today's topic by sharing some trivia about the tongue.

■SEARCH

What James wrote about tongues

Students will discover what James has to say about the tongue.

■REFLECTION

Big damage done by fire, hurricanes—and tongues

This is an opportunity for students to share about times when they've experienced the devastating effects of the tongue, either as the inflicted or the inflictor.

■SOLITUDE

A tongue questionnaire

Students will study other Bible passages concerning the words people use and compare their use of words to God's standards.

■APPLICATION

The power of your tongue

Teens will be able to share about their Solitude and then work as a group to process ways they can keep one another accountable to God's standards concerning their words.

■CLOSING

YOU'LL NEED
Tongue Trivia (pages 69-70)
a whiteboard and markers
Bibles
pens
copies of Faith You Can Say (pages 75-76), one for each student
copies of The Letter—James 3 (pages 147-148), one for each new student
colored pencils

OPENING

After the students have gathered, distribute materials and open the session with prayer. Ask students about applications from the last session. Lead the group in a discussion about the tongue.

Tongue Trivia

▸ *What do you know about your tongue?*

After several have shared, read the following tongue facts to your group.

▸ *Each person has a unique tongue print.*

▸ *The average human has about 10,000 taste buds. However, they're not all on the tongue. Some are under the tongue; some are on the inside of the cheeks; some are on the roof of the mouth. Some can even be found on the lips. These are especially sensitive to salt.*

▸ *Close to 50 percent of the bacteria in the mouth lives on the surface of the tongue.*

▸ *The chameleon has a tongue that's 1.5 times the length of its body. If a human being had a tongue that long, a person five feet tall would have a tongue over seven feet long.*

▸ *In Tibet, it's good manners to stick out your tongue at your guests.*

Transition into the study with a comment something like this:

▸ *All this info focuses on the physical characteristics of the tongue. But have you ever thought about the spiritual impact of your tongue?*

SEARCH

What James wrote about tongues

▸ *The book of James turns from warnings about faith and deeds to a specific application: the tongue. What is a good symbol to use for marking references to the tongue?*

Perhaps a tongue, a mouth, lips, large quotation marks, or a comic-strip word bubble.

▸ *Read The Letter—James 3:1-12. Every time James mentions the tongue, draw one of the suggested symbols around it. When you finish reading and marking, list everything you learn about the tongue on the Faith You Can Say handout. Try to be as detailed as you can.*

After your teens have been working for a few minutes, ask what they have found to be insightful or convicting about the tongue.

Record the responses on the whiteboard and encourage them to write any info they missed in the space provided on their handouts

The tongue is a small part of the body, but it makes great boasts (3:5).

It corrupts the whole person (3:6).

It can set the whole course of a person's life on fire (3:6).

It is itself set on fire by hell (3:6).

It can't be tamed by man (3:8).

It's a restless evil, full of deadly poison (3:8).

We use the same tongue to praise God and curse men, who are made in God's likeness (3:9).

▸ *James uses three great illustrations to show the power of the tongue. What's similar about all these illustrations?*

Something small is controlling something much larger.

SESSION

6

FAITH
YOU CAN
SAY

JAMES
3:1-12

▸ *How is that true of the tongue?*

▸ *Which of these illustrations do you find most descriptive of your own tongue and why?*

▸ *Looking at these verses, can we tell why James needed to address the issue of the tongue with these readers?*

Apparently his readers were cursing men and each other.

REFLECTION

Big damage done by fire, hurricanes—and tongues

Use the following questions to help your students reflect on the damage tongues can do.

▸ *Have you ever seen the tongue spark something like a forest fire?*

▸ *Have you ever been damaged by the fire? Without naming names describe what happened.*

▸ *Has your tongue ever been the spark? What was the result?*

SOLITUDE

A tongue questionnaire

▸ *When you think about it, our entire walk with God—including the picture of God that we project to the world around us—can be seen in only two ways: what we do and what we say. The tongue is responsible for half of our expression of faith. That's probably why James is so emphatic about the subject. And he wasn't the only one!*

▸ *The next exercise is to be done in solitude—just you, your tongue, God, and his Word. Take your handouts and your Bibles to a place where you can listen to God's Spirit as you experience his Word. The instructions for the exercise are printed on your handouts.*

A TONGUE QUESTIONNAIRE

BIBLE PASSAGES	HOW CAN THE TONGUE BE USED DESTRUCTIVELY?	HOW CAN THE TONGUE BE USED CONSTRUCTIVELY?	WHAT IS THE SOURCE OF WHAT THE MOUTH SPEAKS?
PROVERBS 16:28	For gossip. It can separate close friends.		
PROVERBS 17:9	It can repeat an offense and separate close friends.	Or it can promote love by covering over an offense.	
MATTHEW 12:33-37			The mouth speaks out of the overflow of the heart.
ROMANS 10:8-10		We proclaim the word of faith and confess Jesus with our mouth.	
EPHESIANS 4:29	It can speak unwholesome talk.	It can build others up according to their needs and benefit those who may listen.	
EPHESIANS 6:19-20		It can declare fearlessly the mystery of the gospel.	

APPLICATION

The power of your tongue

After about 10 minutes call the group together and discuss questions like these:

▸ *What was the most convicting thing you learned about the tongue?*

▸ *Any volunteers to share how you rated yourself on the scales? Which scale did you score the highest on? Which did you score the lowest on?*

Draw two columns on the board. Label the left column EPHESIANS 4:29 and the right column MATTHEW 12:34.

▸ *Did anybody say yes to these commitments?*

Write the students' names beneath the appropriate reference(s).

▸ *What could happen to our group if we took these verses seriously?*

▸ *How can we hold each other accountable to these commitments?*

SESSION

6

FAITH
YOU CAN
SAY

JAMES
3:1-12

As the students brainstorm on the second question, seek to move them toward a practical plan. You may want to guide the group toward one of the suggestions below.

— **Plaster the Verses**. Find ways to keep the verse references (Ephesians 4:29 and Matthew 12:34) in front of the group. Soap them on mirrors, graffiti them around the youth room, have T-shirts made, create posters. Take advantage of the unique Scripture reference in Matthew: 1-2-3-4.

— **Accountability Partners**. Have the kids form groups of two or three for accountability. Encourage them to phone or e-mail one another daily to check in.

— **Picture Power**. Invite your group members to find an object that represents one of the word pictures James uses to drive his point home. They should display this item wherever they'll see it often to be reminded about using care with their words.

CLOSING

▸ *Earlier we touched on the fact that our entire walk with God—including the picture of God that we project to the world around us—can only be seen in two ways: by what we do and what we say. From the end of James 2 to the beginning of James 3, James hammers away at both of these points.*

▸ *What do you think God is trying to communicate to you through these two truths in James?*

You can let your students ponder this question silently or share their impressions with the group. Close in prayer.

FAITH YOU CAN SAY
James 3:1-12

SEARCH

What James wrote about tongues

Read James 3:1-12. Every time James mentions the tongue, draw a relevant symbol (a tongue, a mouth, lips, large quotation marks, or a comic-strip word bubble) around it. When you finish reading and marking, list everything you learn about the tongue here.

SOLITUDE

A tongue questionnaire

Read the passages in the left column and write in the other columns any information you find that answers the questions in the column headers.

A TONGUE QUESTIONNAIRE

BIBLE PASSAGES	HOW CAN THE TONGUE BE USED DESTRUCTIVELY?	HOW CAN THE TONGUE BE USED CONSTRUCTIVELY?	WHAT IS THE SOURCE OF WHAT THE MOUTH SPEAKS?
PROVERBS 16:28			
PROVERBS 17:9			
MATTHEW 12:33-37			
ROMANS 10:8-10			
EPHESIANS 4:29			
EPHESIANS 6:19-20			

Over the last week, how have you most often used your tongue? Rate yourself on the scales below.

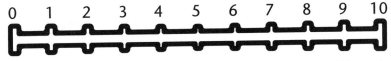

0 1 2 3 4 5 6 7 8 9 10

To talk about people's faults   To cover over people's faults

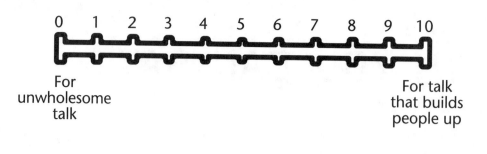

For
unwholesome
talk

For talk
that builds
people up

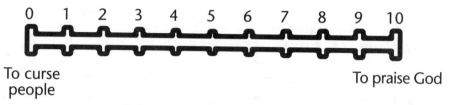

To curse
people

To praise God

Here's what an Ephesians 4:29 commitment looks like:

I will not let any unwholesome talk come out of my mouth.

I will speak only what is helpful for building others up according to their needs.

I will work toward making this a habit over the next ___ days or ___ weeks.

Would you like to commit yourself to Ephesians 4:29?

❏ Yes!　　　　　　❏ I'd like to think about it more.

❏ Not right now.　　❏ No thanks.

Think of at least three people who could use some uplifting words from you. List them.

_____

_____

How about making a Matthew 12:34 commitment? Here's what it looks like:

I will store up only good things in my heart until they overflow into my conversations.

I will begin storing these good things up—

❏ this minute

❏ before today is over

I'll know that I've achieved overflow when I begin to—

❏ Speak more kindly to my family

❏ Speak more kindly to teachers, peers, or coworkers who rub me the wrong way

❏ Talk about Jesus confidently and frequently

❏ No longer feel the need to swear or use bad language

❏ No longer feel the need to lose my temper

❏ Quit pointing out faults in other people

❏ Complain less or not at all

Would you like to commit yourself to Matthew 12:34?

❏ Yes!　　　　　　❏ I'd like to think about it more.

❏ Not right now.　　❏ No thanks.

WISDOM 101
James 3:13-18

The apostle Paul warns in 1 Corinthians 8:1 that knowledge alone won't do us much good. As we study the Bible and encourage students to do the same, we should never forget—nor underestimate—the transformational power of God's Word. Scripture does more than enlarge our base of knowledge. It actually changes us on the inside—which soon shows up on the outside. Read a portion of Psalm 19 below and notice how God's Word (referred to as his law, precepts, ordinances, and so forth) is described. Also note what it has the power to do.

The law of the Lord is perfect, reviving the soul. The statutes of the Lord are trustworthy, making wise the simple. The precepts of the Lord are right, giving joy to the heart. The commands of the Lord are radiant, giving light to the eyes. The fear of the Lord is pure, enduring forever. The ordinances of the Lord are sure and altogether righteous. They are more precious than gold, than much pure gold; they are sweeter than honey, than honey from the comb. By them is your servant warned; in keeping them there is great reward.

—Psalm 19:7-11

One of the benefits listed by the psalmist goes right along with James 3: God's statutes are trustworthy, making wise the simple. Wisdom is something we all want more of. What we forget, however, is that wisdom can come from two directions—above and below. Earthly wisdom looks tempting because it appeals to the flesh and often involves a shortcut. And that's precisely the trap James wants us to avoid.

SEARCH

Good dog, bad dog

Read The Letter—James 3:13-18. As you read, look for two types of wisdom—good wisdom and bad wisdom. Mark each in a unique way.

After you've read and marked the passage, list everything you learn about each type of wisdom.

Good wisdom	Bad wisdom

In verse 17, James lists several behavior traits that accompany wisdom from Heaven. List these in the first column of the following chart. For now, ignore the remaining columns.

BEHAVIOR TRAITS OF WISDOM	SITUATION	SITUATION	SITUATION

He wished for wisdom

Since wisdom is one of the awesome characteristics of God, you might guess that this subject is dealt with in countless Scripture passages. I'll spare you the trouble of looking up all of them (you can thank me later!) and instead focus on just one. Read 1 Kings 3:4-14 from your Bible. As you read, look for answers to the following questions:

What did Solomon ask for?

_____

_____

Why did God like this request?

_____

_____

How did God respond?

_____

_____

You'll recall that James mentions wisdom in an earlier chapter of his letter. Read James 1:5-8 again and answer these questions:

What did James tell us to ask for?

_____

_____

How will God respond?

_____

_____

What similarities or parallels do you see between James' teaching on wisdom and Solomon's request?

REFLECTION

Why God is bullish on wisdom

Based on your study thus far, why do you think God is so pro wisdom?

When it's God's wisdom we're talking about—wisdom from above—what kind of behavior accompanies it?

Why would God want this behavior to be associated with his wisdom?

APPLICATION

Test-drive wisdom (go ahead; take it for a spin)

When you're experiencing a conflict with another person, whose interests do you usually have in mind? If you're completely honest, you'll probably admit that you often place your own interests ahead of the interests of others. Look closely at James 3:14-16. What does this type of "wisdom" degenerate into?

List below any situations in your life (job, ministry, relationships, decisions to make) in which you could use a dose of wisdom from Heaven.

Now look back at the traits that accompany heavenly wisdom. You listed them in the chart at the beginning of this lesson. Here's an example of how you can evaluate your situation by those traits: Let's say you're the youth director of a church, and you'd like to do a major outreach event. You've already done some legwork to bring in a band and a speaker and to offer loads of food. Since your church has never done something of this magnitude, not everyone is supportive of your idea. In fact, you're encountering some resistance. You're unsure how to proceed—but luckily you've studied James 3. What questions can you ask to evaluate the situation by each trait?

PREP IT PREP IT PREP IT PREP IT PREP IT PREP IT PREP IT PREP IT

TEST-DRIVE WISDOM (GO AHEAD; TAKE IT FOR A SPIN)

WISDOM TRAIT	EVALUATE
PEACE-LOVING	When you imagine meeting with key board members or staff on this subject, do you picture a confrontation? Have you thought about how you can share your vision without being combative?
CONSIDERATE	Stephen R. Covey says, "Seek first to understand, then to be understood (*The Seven Habits of Highly Effective People*, 1989). A great maxim! Are you being quick to listen and slow to speak (James 1:19)?
SUBMISSIVE	Do you have the support of your pastoral leadership? Are you operating in submission to those who have authority over you?
FULL OF MERCY	If the event happens and is a huge success, will you in any way communicate a "See? I told you so!" attitude? Will you view success as an opportunity to advance your agenda?
FULL OF GOOD FRUIT	As you interact with those who are resistant to your ideas, will they leave your presence affirmed and encouraged in their walk with Jesus? Or will they head home to reload for the next confrontation?
IMPARTIAL	Are you open to the possibility that you may be wrong?
SINCERE	Do you have the support of your pastoral leadership? Are you operating in submission to those who have authority over you?
PURE	What are your motives? Are they pure? Are you planning this event out of a broken heart for the lost and obedience to a prompting from God? Are you privately pleased about the increase of your personal visibility or the praise for your ministry or program?

Now it's your turn to give it a spin. In the chart at the beginning of this lesson, write three of your situations in the column headings. Then apply the traits of godly wisdom to each situation, just as we did in the sample. Let the Holy Spirit teach you through this exercise; there may be a thing or two he's been itching to say!

Finally, note the promise in James 3:18—in fact, write it below.

Just ask!

As you wrap up, consider this question: Has this study brought to mind any recent times when you acted out of earthly wisdom? If so, remember that God loves a repentant heart. Before you meet with your students, get right with God and others. Ask the forgiveness of anyone you've dealt with out of earthly wisdom.

Before the group session, be sure to read through Teach It so you're familiar with the session and can lead it comfortably.

One option for the next session's closing (page 96) requires a little extra preparation. Look at it now so you have time to pull together a few resources if you choose that option.

WISDOM 101
James 3:13-18

■ OPENING

Introduce the word *wisdom* and give students an opportunity
to define it.

■ SEARCH

Good dog, bad dog
Students will discover the two types of wisdom discussed in
James 3.

■ REFLECTION

Why God is bullish on wisdom
This exercise will allow students to compare the wisdom
described in James 3 with Solomon's wisdom.

■ APPLICATION

Test-drive wisdom (go ahead; take it for a spin)
Students will apply the behavioral traits that accompany godly
wisdom to life's situations.

■ CLOSING

Just ask!
Give teens an opportunity to do what James told us to do—ask
God for wisdom.

YOU'LL NEED
a whiteboard and markers
Bibles
pens
copies of Wisdom 101 (pages 85-86), one for each student
copies of The Letter—James 3 (pages 147-148), one for each new student
colored pencils

Students who were present for the last session should use the copies of James 3 they have already marked.

OPENING

When the group has gathered, distribute materials and open the session with prayer. Check in
with your teens about how they're doing on applications from the last session.

Turn the discussion to the word *wisdom*. As you read each question below, ask the group members to write a response on their Wisdom 101 handouts before discussing it as a group.

▸ *How would you define wisdom?*

▸ *What's the difference between intelligence and wisdom?*

▸ *If you had to choose, which would you rather have: wisdom or intelligence?*

Good dog, bad dog

▶ *You could probably make the case that wisdom is the application—the practical how-to—of knowledge. And since application is James' middle name, you can bet he won't leave any application stones unturned.*

▶ *Using The Letter, read James 3:13-18. As you read, circle what James says about wisdom that comes from Heaven and underline what he says about the other kind of wisdom.*

After five minutes, ask your kids what they learned about wisdom that comes from heaven. As you write the responses on the board, draw out the following points:

Wisdom is shown by a good life (3:13).

It drives deeds done in humility (3:13).

It's pure, peace loving, considerate, submissive, full of mercy and good fruit, impartial, and sincere (3:17).

You may want to give your kids the dictionary definition of wisdom and wise to transition into the session.

Now ask what they learned about the other kind of wisdom.

It's earthly, unspiritual (3:15).

Its true source is the Devil (3:15).

It's accompanied by envy, selfish ambition, disorder, and every evil practice (3:16).

"Wisdom"
— Insightful understanding of what is true, right or enduring
— Native good judgment

"Wise"
— Having great learning
— Having discernment: sagacious
— Sensible
—Prudent

▶ *Based on these verses, how can we know if we're operating out of God's wisdom, our own wisdom, or the Devil's wisdom?*

Each type of wisdom leads to its own type of behavior.

▶ *James 3:17 gives a list of behavior traits that accompany God's wisdom. Take a minute to copy these in the first column of the chart on your Wisdom 101 handout*

▶ *Flip to James 1:5. What else did James says about wisdom?*

If you lack wisdom, ask God, who gives it generously.

▶ *If you don't believe James 1:5, there's a guy in the Bible who put this promise to the test. Read 1 Kings 3:4-14 in your Bible. Then answer the questions about it on your handout.*

Why God is bullish on wisdom

Give the students about five minutes to read this passage and write their responses on their handouts.

▸ *What did Solomon ask for?*

He asked for a discerning heart to govern God's people and distinguish between right and wrong (1 Kings 3:9).

▸ *Why did God like this request?*

Because it wasn't a selfish prayer for a perfect life but a selfless prayer asking for the ability to perform the duties God had given him (1 Kings 3:11).

▸ *How did God respond?*

God gave him what he asked for and much more (1 Kings 3:12-14).

▸ *What similarities do you see between Solomon's situation and what James wrote?*

Wisdom was given generously to Solomon.

God's wisdom isn't self-serving.

God's wisdom translates into humble behavior.

▸ *Why do you think God is so pro wisdom?*

When God's people use his wisdom, they reflect his all-wise character and accomplish his will.

▸ *We defined wisdom at the beginning of the session. What could we add to our definition based on what we've seen in Scripture?*

Let the group members process what it means to have wisdom, ultimately steering the discussion to these definitions:

Wisdom is an ability to use good judgment and discernment in making decisions and resolving conflicts.

It shows up in a good life, humble deeds, and godly behavior.

It's not magical intelligence from God to pass a math test! It's discerning right from wrong in situations where it's not so obvious.

> ▸ *What are some situations you or your friends face in which God's wisdom would really help?*

Friendships	*Dating relationships*
Conflicts with parents	*Major decisions (choosing a college or career)*

APPLICATION

Test-drive wisdom (go ahead; take it for a spin)

> ▸ *In the chart at the beginning of your handout, write two or three situations where you could use a dose of wisdom from God.*

> ▸ *Spend the next few minutes applying God's wisdom to these situations. In other words, ask yourself how you could use each behavior trait listed in the chart to make a decision, resolve a conflict, or whatever your situation entails. Ask God to show you how each trait applies to your particular situation.*

To clarify this exercise, share the example from your leader preparation—or tailor an example to a situation your students have likely faced. You may want to ask your teens to find a place where they can be alone with God to do this exercise.

After about 10 minutes, call the students back together.

> ▸ *What kinds of situations did you list? Were they school-related? Family-related? Friends? Work?*

> ▸ *If you feel inadequate to resolve your situations or make good decisions, what did James say to do?*

> *Ask God for wisdom.*

CLOSING

Just ask!

> ▸ *Since God generously gives wisdom to those who ask for it, the best thing we can do right now is ask! In our closing minutes spend some time in prayer, asking for wisdom about the personal situations you've noted. Pray that you will exhibit the behavior traits from James 3:17 as you act on the wisdom you receive.*

OPTION

Divide the students into smaller groups of two or three. Have the students pray for each other's needs.

OPTION

Compile a master list of the students' situations. Ask each student to select a behavior trait to focus on as they pray. For example, one student could pray about "good fruit" in all the situations on the master list.

OPTION

Ask the students to journal a prayer asking for wisdom. Have them keep this prayer handy and pray it every day for a week.

WISDOM 101
James 3:13-18

How would you define wisdom?

_____

_____

What's the difference between intelligence and wisdom?

_____

_____

If you had to choose, which would you rather have: wisdom or intelligence?

_____

_____

Good dog, bad dog

In the first column list behavior traits in James 3:17. Later you'll come back to the other columns to follow your leader's directions.

TEST-DRIVE WISDOM
(go ahead; take it for a spin)

BEHAVIOR TRAITS OF WISDOM	SITUATION	SITUATION	SITUATION

85

Why God is bullish on wisdom

Read 1 Kings 3:4-14 from your Bible. As you read, look for the answers to the following questions.

What did Solomon ask for?

_____

_____

_____

_____

_____

_____

Why did God like this request?

_____

_____

_____

_____

_____

_____

How did God respond?

_____

_____

_____

_____

_____

_____

_____

SANCTUARY
James 4:1-12

Authentic spiritual strength—with all its by-products—comes from lingering, intimate times with the Lord. A schedule packed with activity (even ministry) will deprive us from experiencing Jesus' living water where it flows the strongest and most pure. We may actually become addicted to our busyness, and, before long, the things of the world may become more and more enticing.

The author of Hebrews, as evidenced in the passage below, understood this truth. As you read the following verses, note how rest from busyness provides opportunity to receive maximum impact from the Word of God.

There remains, then, a Sabbath-rest for the people of God; for anyone who enters God's rest also rests from his own work, just as God did from his. Let us, therefore, make every effort to enter that rest, so that no one will fall by following their example of disobedience. For the word of God is living and active. Sharper than any double-edged sword, it penetrates even to dividing soul and spirit, joints and marrow; it judges the thoughts and attitudes of the heart.
—Hebrews 4:9-12

The second option for concluding the session with your teens (page 96) requires some advanced preparation. Take a look early so you have time to pull together a few resources if you choose that option.

Take a deep breath and release your grip on this day and its activities. You're about to hear James expound on a point similar to this one from Hebrews. But don't think of this study time as preparation for ministry activity (leading your students). Think of it as a lingering, intimate time with the Savior. Enter his rest and give his Word maximum opportunity to penetrate your heart.

SEARCH

We've got a few problems here...

Read The Letter—James 4:1-12. Circle every reference to the readers of the letter.

Once you've read and marked the passage, look back at what you circled. Note the problems James' readers were experiencing.

_____

_____

In James 4:7-10 we see a series of instructions and promises. Reread the passage, underlining the instructions in one color and the promises in another. Then list each instruction and the promise that comes with it.

_____

_____

If the instructions and promises are offered as solutions to the problems (which is likely), what connection do you see between the problems mentioned in James 4:1-4 and the instructions and promises in verses 7-10?

_____

_____

...Then you walked into the sanctuary

Do you sense that James is asking his readers to refocus their eyes on things are truly important? When we lose our intensity in following Jesus, our default settings tend to take over: selfish desires, earthly ambitions, longing for the things of the world rather than the things of God.

The author of Psalm 73, a Hebrew priest, had a similar problem. Read Psalm 73 twice from your Bible (it's short—just 28 verses). In your first read through, note the turning point that Asaph, the writer, experiences. Draw a lightning bolt over this verse in your Bible.

As you read the psalm a second time, list everything that describes Asaph and his perception of the world before the turning point and after the turning point.

Before	After

What happens to Asaph between the before and the after? Write it word for word.

_____

_____

What similarities do you see between Asaph before his turning point and James' readers in James 4:1-4?

_____

_____

In what ways do the instructions and promises of James 4:7-10 show up in Psalm 73? Be specific.

_____

_____

How is your story similar to Asaph's? Are you involved in ministry as Asaph was but not getting any true sanctuary time with God? Do you have moments when the things of the world look fulfilling—when you can't even remember why you're supposed to resist them?

_____

_____

Your marching orders: submit, resist, come near—and lose that pride

Perhaps James' instructions in verses 7-10 can serve as a basis for establishing real sanctuary time with God: submit to God, resist the Devil, come near to God, purify your heart, humble yourself. If we do these things, the Word promises that the Devil will flee, and God will come near and lift us up. That's a good deal! But our part of the equation is to obey the instructions.

List two or three things you can do to incorporate these instructions into your daily routine.

Submit to God and resist the Devil.

_____

_____

Come near to God.

_____

_____

Humble yourself before the Lord.

_____

_____

What are some areas of your life where genuine sanctuary time with God would be helpful? How would you like to experience the promises outlined in James 4? Listed below are several areas for personal meditation and prayer. Think about how you might apply the instructions from James to each area as you write your impressions.

My signature sins and temptations

_____

_____

My prayer life

_____

_____

Decision making

_____

_____

Personal Bible study

_____

_____

Building relationships

_____

_____

Other

_____

_____

Read through Teach It so you're familiar with it. Be sure to note the cues for recording the information on the board. The second option for concluding the session will take some advanced preparation, depending on how involved you make the exercise.

SESSION 8
SANCTUARY
James 4:1-12

■ OPENING

This agree/disagree discussion will introduce the subject of the session—seeking sanctuary time with God.

■ SEARCH

We've got a few problems here...
Students will uncover the struggles faced by James' audience and solutions offered to overcome them.

■ SOLITUDE

...Then you walked into the sanctuary
Students will investigate how a priest of Israel overcame the same struggles as those faced by James' readers.

■ REFLECTION

...And on the keyboard, let's hear it for Asaph!
This exercise will allow students to compare their personal experiences with those of the psalmist and James' audience.

■ APPLICATION

Your marching orders: submit, resist, come near—and lose that pride
In this exercise the group will brainstorm practical ways in which they can obey James' instructions and experience sanctuary with God.

■ CLOSING

Finding one's own sanctuary

■ OPTION

This is an opportunity for teens to experience a personal sanctuary time, either during the session or later at home.

■ OPTION

Experience sanctuary as a group.

YOU'LL NEED

a whiteboard and markers

Bibles

pens

copies of Sanctuary (page 97-98), one for each student

copies of The Letter—James 4 (page 148-149), one for each new student

colored pencils

worship CDs, CD player, selected Scriptures on transparencies or PowerPoint, projection system (optional)

After the students have gathered, distribute materials and open the session with prayer. Let your students share about their applications from other sessions. Introduce the subject of today's study with the following discussion.

▶ *Do you agree or disagree with this statement: "If Satan can't make you sin, he'll make you busy"? Why do you think that?*

▶ *Why would Satan care if we're busy? What if we're busy doing good things?*

We've got a few problems here...

▶ *If our busy schedules rob us of the one thing that gives us strength and perspective—intimacy with God—then we've been rendered as ineffective as if we lived a sinful life. Our natural tendency toward selfishness kicks in, and before long we're more worried about our own agenda than God's agenda.*

▶ *James gives us some insight on how we can avoid this problem. Read The Letter—James 4:1-12. Circle every reference to the readers of James.*

While the group reads the passage, make three columns on the board. Leave a blank space at the top of each column for a heading. When you and your students have finished this lesson, the chart will look something like this. You'll walk through the process of creating this chart with your students during the lesson.

WE'VE GOT A FEW PROBLEMS HERE...

BEFORE	SANCTUARY	AFTER
JAMES' READERS	INSTRUCTIONS	PROMISES
QUARRELLING AND FIGHTING (4:1)	RESIST THE DEVIL (4:7)	THE DEVIL WILL FLEE FROM YOU (4:7)
NOT PRAYING (4:2)	COME NEAR TO GOD (4:8)	GOD WILL COME NEAR TO YOU (4:8)
PRAYING FOR THINGS THEY WANTED FOR THEIR OWN PLEASURE (4:3)	HUMBLE YOURSELF BEFORE THE LORD (4:10)	HE WILL LIFT YOU UP (4:10)
FRIENDSHIP WITH THE WORLD (4:4)		
SLANDERING ONE ANOTHER (4:11)		
ASAPH		ASAPH
ASAPH WAS A PRIEST WHO WAS ABOUT TO CHECK OUT; HE WANTED NOTHING MORE TO DO WITH GOD.		ASAPH NOW WANTED NOTHING TO DO WITH THE WORLD AND EVERYTHING TO DO WITH GOD.
HE WAS TEMPTED BY THE GREENER GRASS ON THE OTHER SIDE OF THE FENCE.		HE SAW THROUGH THE DECEPTIONS THAT WERE TEMPTING HIM EARLIER.
HE WAS OPPRESSED BY WHAT HE WAS FEELING.		HE SEEMS AT PEACE.

After about five minutes have the students look back at what they circled.

▸ *From the looks of it, what were some of the problems James' readers were facing?*

Record the students' responses in the first column on the board.

▸ *How would you characterize this group of people generally?*

Sinful. Self-centered. They sound a lot like many of today's churches or youth groups!

▸ *To counteract these problems James gives a series of instructions and promises. Reread James 4:7-10, this time underlining all the instructions in one color and the promises in another.*

After about five minutes, ask—

▸ *Look at what you've underlined in James 4:7-10. There are several instructions, but in some cases there's a promise attached to him. Which instructions come with a promise?*

Record the instructions in the middle column and the promises in the right column. Note the link between each instruction and promise with an arrow.

▸ *Think back to the problems James' readers were experiencing. What do you think the impact would be if they had obeyed these instructions and received these promises?*

— *They might be praying more.*
— *Their prayers would be more humble (for the right things with the right motives).*
— *They wouldn't be fighting and quarreling.*
— *They would give up their self-serving attitude and replace it with a God-serving attitude.*

SOLITUDE

...Then you walked into the sanctuary

▸ *When we lose our intensity about seeking Jesus, our default settings tend to take over. We get selfish in our desires and ambitions, and we want the things of the world more than the things of God. No one is exempt from this—not me, not you, not even the guys who wrote the Bible! In fact, the writer of one of the psalms, a Hebrew priest, had the same problem.*

Invite the students to do the first section of their Sanctuary handout in solitude. They can stay where they are or take their Bibles and handouts to a more private spot. The instructions for the exercise are printed on the handout.

...And on the keyboard, let's hear it for Asaph!

After about 15 minutes call the group back together and discuss Psalm 73.

▸ *How would you describe Asaph at the beginning of the psalm?*

▸ *How would you describe Asaph at the end of the psalm?*

Add the answers to the first question in the first column (under the problems of James' readers) and the answers to the second question in the third column. Label the first column BEFORE and the third column AFTER.

▸ *What made the difference? What was the turning point for Asaph?*

He entered the sanctuary of God.

Now label the middle column SANCTUARY. The board should now look similar to the completed chart at the beginning of the lesson.

Your marching orders: submit, resist, come near—and lose that pride

▸ *What inferences can we make from this information about following God?*

We need sanctuary experiences with God to help us see through the deceptions of temptation and selfishness.

Without the experience of God's presence we revert to our default settings; we pursue selfish desires and what looks like pleasure.

With the experience of God's presence we receive strength to beat our temptations and enjoy a close walk with God.

▸ *Have you ever experienced this in your own life?*

Let the students share openly about their losses in battling temptation, as well as their victories when they've had true encounters with God. You can set the tone by sharing yourself as well.

▸ *How can regular sanctuary times keep us from being like James' readers and Asaph in the Before column? How do they help us be like the obedient Christians and Asaph in the After column?*

When we regularly receive strength and wisdom from intimacy with God, our selfish desires become less important, and God's desires become more important. Regular time with God gives him an opportunity to pour himself into us. The more God we have in us, the less of a grip the world will have on us.

▶ *James gives three clear-cut instructions that come with promises. What are some practical things we could do to obey these instructions and enjoy the promises?*

Submit to God/Resist the Devil: Choose TV programs, movies, magazines, and music, wisely. Avoid being alone at home with a boyfriend or girlfriend.

Come Near to God: Spend 20, 30 or 60 minutes each day for the next week reading the Bible and praying. The next time there's a day off from school, spend a longer time (half or whole day) with God. Choose a fast food or leisure activity to use as a reminder for a week to spend a few moments in prayer.

Humble Yourself before the Lord: Adopt a posture of humility when praying, such as kneeling. Focus on minimizing the words I, my, *or* me *during prayer.*

CLOSING

Finding one's own sanctuary

OPTION

Give the students an opportunity for some personal sanctuary time with God, using the last portion of the handout. If there's still time, students can have this sanctuary time as part of the session. If not, they can take the handouts home to do them. Whether they have Sanctuary time-during your session or at home, encourage your students to use these passages to seek their own sanctuary experience with God.

OPTION

Whether you're meeting in a home or at church, whether you play an instrument or a CD, you can lead your group in a communal sanctuary experience. If your group is comfortable with it, change the atmosphere by lowering the lights, lighting candles, and moving to throw pillows on the floor.

Spend time worshiping through music.

If you have video or overhead projection capability, project some of these verses of Scripture as the music plays.

Submit to God/Resist the Devil: Romans 6:13; 1 Peter 5:6-10

Come Near to God: Deuteronomy 4:29-31; Jeremiah 29:13; Hebrews 11:6

Humble Yourself: Luke 14:7-14; Luke 18:9-14

Give the group plenty of time for meditative prayer. You may want to include dance or other creative arts.

Two resources published by Youth Specialties can help you: The Book of Uncommon Prayer: Contemplative and Celebratory Prayers and Worship Services for Youth Ministry *by Steve Case (2002) and* Worship Services for Youth Groups: 12 Complete Thematic and Seasonal Services *by Jim Marian (1996).*

SANCTUARY
James 4:1-12

SOLITUDE

...Then you walked into the sanctuary

Read Psalm 73 twice from your Bible (it's short—only 28 verses). During your first read, look for the turning point that Asaph, the writer of the psalm, experiences. Draw a lightning bolt over this verse in your Bible.

As you read the psalm a second time, list everything that describes Asaph and his perception of the world before the turning point and after the turning point.

Before	After

What happens to Asaph between the before and the after? In other words, what was his turning point? Write it word for word.

What similarities do you see between Asaph before his turning point and James' readers in James 4:1-4?

Compare Asaph after his turning point with the instructions and promises you saw in James 4:7-10. In what ways does Asaph enjoy the same promises James describes? Be as specific as possible.

Where do you fit? Rate yourself on the Asaph scale.

Asaph before   Asaph after

0   1   2   3   4   5   6   7   8   9   10

I constantly cave in to the temptations around me

I receive strength from God and consistently beat the temptations around me.

Finding one's own sanctuary

If your leader directs you to, find a place where you can get alone with God—your own sanctuary with him. Use these Scriptures to get started. Interact with God about them. Journal what you learn about submitting, resisting, drawing near to God, and humbling yourself.

Submit to God/Resist the Devil

Romans 6:13

1 Peter 5:6-10

_____

_____

Come near to God

Deuteronomy 4:29-31

Jeremiah 29:13

_____

_____

Hebrews 11:6

_____

_____

Humble yourself

Luke 14:7-14

Luke 18:9-14

_____

_____

SESSION

9

THE TIME
OF YOUR
LIFE

JAMES
4:13-17

SESSION 9

THE TIME OF YOUR LIFE
James 4:13-17

My frame was not hidden from you when I was made in the secret place. When I was woven together in the depths of the earth, your eyes saw my unformed body. All the days ordained for me were written in your book before one of them came to be.

—Psalm 139:15-16

God ordained all of your days—even before the day of your conception! That means that he chose your ordained days to be now, at this particular point in history. Have you ever noticed how certain people have used their precise time in history to great advantage? For example, would we recognize the name Beethoven if he'd been born before the invention of the piano? Or Jordan before the birth of basketball? Or Gates before the integrated circuit?

Is it possible that you were meant to use your ordained days to similar advantage? Let that question bounce around in your mind as you study what James—and ultimately God—has to say on the subject.

SEARCH

Watching time go by

Under some conditions life seems short. At other times life seems long. Under all conditions life is limited. We've each received a set number of days at a particular point in history. And we've each been given an opportunity to observe God's creation during a short span of what we know as *time.*

In chapter 4, James makes a quick detour from his previous subject and gives a brief discourse on the subject of time. It's just five verses, but James is emphatic in what he says. In fact, he introduces the subject with the words, "Now listen." We should!

Read The Letter—James 4:13-17. As you read, draw a clock over every reference to time and underline any references to life.

After you've read and marked the passage, answer the following questions.

What does the passage teach us about "tomorrow"?

_____

_____

What does it teach us about life?

_____

_____

What instruction does James give to teach us what to do with the time we've been given?

_____

_____

To plan or not to plan?

James describes life as a mist (4:14). Think about your life as a mist for a moment. Compare the way you plan your life to James' examples. Are you more like the person described in verse 13 or the one described in verse 15?

_____

_____

If you're more like the person in 4:13, do you boast or brag about your plans? If you're thinking, "Nah, I'd never do that," consider how you communicate your goals or vision of ministry.

_____

_____

Jesus on time

It's worth our time to check out Jesus' teaching on life and how to use it. Read Luke 12:22-31 from your Bible.

What does Jesus tell us not to worry about?

_____

_____

What does he tell us to worry about? (key word: *seek*.)

_____

_____

What parallels can you draw between "knowing the good you ought to do" in James 4:17 and "seeking his kingdom" Luke 12:31?

_____

_____

Some people get guilt-trip chills down their spines when they hear the phrase "sins of omission." They may be tempted to rationalize the guilt away: "I can't be held responsible for all the good I might have done but didn't." But Scripture says otherwise. As you read the passages below, record what you learn about not doing the good you're supposed to do.

SESSION
9

THE TIME
OF YOUR
LIFE

JAMES
4:13-17

PROVERBS 3:27-28

_____

_____

MATTHEW 7:26-27

_____

_____

MATTHEW 25:41-46

_____

_____

LUKE 12:42-48

_____

_____

BACKGROUND

The peril of presuming

James touches on one specific sin in a backhanded way. You won't be focusing on this sin in the group session, but as the leader, you'll benefit from this background study.

Sins of Presumption

The sin of presumption weaves its way through the entire Bible. What is this little-known sin? It's when we presume to know what God will say or do—when in reality, we don't know. We dabble in this sin when we assert what God prefers in such things as worship style, vision of ministry, and God's will about many matters he has not specifically addressed in his Word. This may make more sense when you read a few examples in Scripture. (Is it coincidental that in the Bible the spiritual leaders were most susceptible to sins of presumption?)

NUMBERS 14:42-45

_____

_____

DEUTERONOMY 18:20

_____

_____

PSALM 19:13

_____

_____

1 PETER 4:11

_____

_____

Take a minute to journal your thoughts (or perhaps write a prayer) regarding two possible responses to the sin of presumption:

Is there anything for which you need to repent or ask forgiveness? If so, what?

_____

_____

Would you like to make a commitment similar to David's in Psalm 19:13?

_____

Time is short—so watch those priorities!

Back to James 4:13-17. Let's see if these five little verses can help us make better use of the time we've been given.

First, a couple of facts:

— Your life is a mist.   — The mist appears for a little while and then vanishes.

Now a couple of questions:

What did James say to do in the brief time in which your misty life exists?

_____

_____

Look back at Luke 12:31. What did Jesus say to do in the brief time you've been given?

_____

_____

Now for the hard stuff:

Are you willing to submit your calendar, your checkbook, your priorities, and your pursuits to the phrase "if it is the Lord's will" (James 4:15)?

_____

_____

Are you willing to live by the phrase, "I don't even know what will happen tomorrow" (James 4:14) if it means loosening your grip on things that give you security and comfort? If your answer is yes, in what areas do you need to loosen your grip?

_____

_____

How can you adjust your schedule to allow for "spontaneous good"—the good you know you ought to do but rarely have time for?

_____

_____

Seize the day!

Why wait till you're with your students to begin applying James 4:13-17? Think now about the good things you ought to do. Now do it. Before today is over. (Remember, your life is a mist.)

After you've done the good things that came to mind, take a minute to read over Teach It. Give some thought to the Application; you'll want to suggest ideas as your students consider the good they ought to do.

THE TIME OF YOUR LIFE
James 4:13-17

■ OPENING

Introduce the subject of our personal life spans by sharing trivia about life spans in general.

■ SEARCH

Watching time go by

Students will discover in James 4 what we should do with our fleeting life spans.

■ SOLITUDE

Jesus on time

Students will search out related Scriptures to complete the picture of what to do with the life span we're given.

■ APPLICATION

Time is short—so watch those priorities!

Teens will be encouraged to get specific (and intense!) about the good they should do.

■ CLOSING

If your group meets early in the day, take action today.

YOU'LL NEED

a whiteboard and markers

Bibles

pens

copies of The Time of Your Life (pages 107-108), one for each student

copies of The Letter—James 4 (pages 148-149), one for each new student

colored pencils

Students who were present for the last session should use the copies of James 4 they have already marked.

OPENING

After the group has gathered, distribute materials and open the session with prayer. Follow up with your teens to see how they've been doing on their recent applications.

Share some of the following trivia regarding the life span.

Did you know that—

▸ *In 1900 the average human life span was 50 years; by 1940 it was 65. Today the average is almost 80 years.*

TEACH IT TEACH IT TEACH IT TEACH IT TEACH IT TEACH IT TEACH IT

▶ The average life span of a fifth-century man living in England was 30 years.

▶ The average life span of a human taste bud is seven to 10 days.

▶ The average human eyelash lives about 150 days.

▶ Beards are the fastest-growing hairs on the human body. If the average man never trimmed his beard, it would grow to nearly 30 feet in his lifetime.

▶ The average human heart beats about 100,000 times every 24 hours. In a 72-year lifetime, the heart beats more than 2.5 billion times.

▶ Between ages 30 and 70 a human nose may lengthen and widen by as much as half an inch and the ears may grow a quarter-inch longer. (Why? Because cartilage is one of the few tissues that continue to grow as we age.)

Watching time go by

Segue into the study with comments something like this:

▶ So other than growing taste buds and eyelashes, what are we supposed to do with the life span we've been given? Today we're studying just five verses in James. But this one little paragraph could impact how each of us uses the life span we've been given.

▶ Using The Letter, read James 4:13-17. As you read, draw a clock above every reference to time and underline references to life.

After your kids have spent two or three minutes on this passage, ask—

▶ What does James tell us about tomorrow?

We don't know what will happen.

▶ What does James teach us about life?

It's like a mist.
A mist evaporates quickly and unpredictably.

▶ How would you sum up what James is saying in these verses?

As the students discuss the question, focus their attention on James 4:17. Since life is fleeting and uncertain, we shouldn't pass up an opportunity to do the good we know we ought to do.

Jesus on time

SESSION
9

THE TIME
OF YOUR
LIFE

JAMES
4:13-17

▸ *James isn't the only one in the Bible who tells us to be less consumed with our priorities and more consumed with God's. For the next few minutes, you'll be spending time with some words from Jesus. Some of these passages may be familiar but make an effort to read them as if you're hearing them for the first time.*

Ask the students to move to a place where they can get comfortable for some solitude time with God. They'll need their handouts—where they'll find the directions—their Bibles, and The Letter.

Time is short—so watch those priorities!

After about 15 minutes, call the group back together. Ask the students to share any Wow! moments they experienced. After some have shared, draw a timeline near the top of the white-board and discuss the following questions.

Birth   Death

▸ *We each have a limited time—like a mist—to do the good we know we ought to do. Based on what Jesus says about worry in Luke 12, what are some things we can let go of that will help us focus on seeking his kingdom? Such as...*

Worrying about their looks   *Buying the popular music*

Having the right clothes   *Mindless leisure*

Write the students' responses below the timeline on the board. Ask them to record these below the timeline on their handouts.

▸ *What good can we be doing around us for "the least of these"?*

Clean out our closets this Saturday and take the decent clothes to a homeless shelter.

Contribute $10 (or other sacrificial amount) each for a shopping spree at a discount food store. Take the food to a church food pantry.

Here are two ideas to get your kids thinking. Write the students' responses below the timeline on the board, and encourage them to record this info beneath the timelines on their handouts.

Seize the day!

If your group meets early in the day, you may want to move from Bible study right into "doing the good you ought to do." (After all, your life span is limited; why not start *now*?) You could collect money on the spot for a grocery spree and do the shopping now. Or challenge each student to have two sacks of clothing ready to give away by the time they go to bed tonight.

Close the session with group prayer. Ask any volunteers to pray aloud for the Lord's leading concerning "the good we ought to do."

THE TIME OF YOUR LIFE
James 4:13-17

SESSION

9

THE TIME
OF YOUR
LIFE

JAMES
4:13-17

SOLITUDE

Jesus on time

The next thought may seem morbid to some people, but it's absolutely true: Just as your life has a starting point, it will have an ending point. What that means is that unless Jesus returns before you die, there will be two dates on your tombstone—your birth and your death. So on the time-line below, write your birthday. Then continue with the exercises that follow.

__/__/__

Birth   Death

LUKE 12:22-31	MATTHEW 7:26-27	MATTHEW 25:41-46	LUKE 12:42-48

What to do with the time of your life

Read the first passage listed above, Luke 12:22-31. List in the chart all the things Jesus tells us not to focus on. Then jot down one thing Jesus tells us we should focus on.

_____

_____

THE TIME OF YOUR LIFE: JAMES 4:13-17

What *not* to do with the time of your life

After reading James 4:17 you may be saying, "But I can't be responsible for all the good I should do and don't do!" But the Bible says something else. Read the verses in the second, third, and fourth columns. Write down what Jesus says about passing up opportunities to do good.

Did you notice that the stakes for following Jesus just got a little higher?

What about the time of your life?

One of three things will happen tomorrow. Either you'll live, Jesus will return, or you'll die. James is saying that if you wake up tomorrow and find yourself alive, you should live as if the other two things are really going to happen—*because they will*!

James says our attitude should be, "If it's the Lord's will, we will live and do this or that." Evaluate your attitude. Consider each of the following areas:

Your calendar

How could you change your schedule to be available to do "spontaneous good"—whenever the Lord puts it in your path? How might you pare down your activities, so that you never miss an opportunity to do the good you ought to do? Write three changes or adjustments you could make.

_____

_____

Your priorities

Who's in control of your priorities?

❏ Me   ❏ God

It's easy to check a box with the right answer, but how about living it? What would your career choice look like if God were in control? Write down two ideas about how you could let the Lord control and direct your career path.

_____

_____

Now think about how you spend your free time. Does it measure up to James 4:13-17? If not, what are two ways you'd like to change?

_____

_____

Your needs and concerns

What do you worry about most? Make a list. Are any of them things Jesus said not to worry about? Write down three things you could loosen your grip on, in order to tighten your grip on seeking Jesus and his kingdom.

_____

_____

IT'S NOT JUST THE MONEY
James 5:1-11

SESSION
10

IT'S NOT
JUST THE
MONEY

JAMES
5:1-11

Money is one of the top five topics addressed in Scripture, receiving almost as much attention as the subject of love. But when you read carefully what God says about money, you'll see that money itself is not the problem, but the effect of money. Some of the godliest people in Scripture—Job and Abraham, to name two—had immense wealth, even by the world's standards.

The problem is that the world's wealth can make us less dependent on God, who is the source of all we have in the first place. Listen to the words God speaks through Moses just before his people enter the Promised Land.

When the Lord your God brings you into the land he swore to your fathers, to Abraham, Isaac and Jacob, to give you—a land with large, flourishing cities you did not build, houses filled with all kinds of good things you did not provide, wells you did not dig, and vineyards and olive groves you did not plant—then when you eat and are satisfied, be careful that you do not forget the Lord, who brought you out of Egypt, out of the land of slavery...Be sure to keep the commands of the Lord your God and the stipulations and decrees he has given you.

—Deuteronomy 6:10-12, 17

The Lord desires that our behavior be driven by dependence on him. He trusts his Word—his commands, stipulations, and decrees—to keep us dependent. Perhaps we should trust it too. James 5 is a great place to start.

SEARCH

Get the big picture of this chapter

Read The Letter—James 5:1-11. As you read, circle every reference to the readers of the letter. In a different color underline every reference to the Lord.

After you've read and marked the passage, review what you've underlined and list what you learn about the Lord. You'll notice that James uses the title Lord for both Jesus and God. Try to distinguish between the Lord Jesus and the Lord God as you make your list.

_____

_____

_____

As you've studied the book of James, you may have noticed that James often refers to his readers as "my brothers." In James 5:1 what group of people is he singling out?

_____

_____

James reserves some of his best word pictures for his warnings to the rich. Reread James 5:1-6 and draw a box around the word pictures he uses to depict the situation of the rich. List them.

_____

_____

In light of the fact that "the Lord's coming is near," James encourages his readers to have a particular attitude. Reread James 5:7-11 and record below the instructions concerning this attitude.

_____

_____

BACKGROUND
Murder!

James accuses the rich of a pretty intense action toward the poor in verse 6—murder. Commentators speculate that he is referring to the result of the rich cheating the poor out of their only means of income—their land. Without livelihood or sustenance the poor literally starved to death.

REFLECTION
Harsh words for the rich

So who were these rich people in James 5? At first glance, you might assume James was addressing the rich who were part of the Christian community he was writing to—the 12 tribes scattered among the nations. Many scholars believe these rich people were outside the Christian community and that James was warning them in defense of his primary audience. (In James 2:5-7 we learned that James' readers were being exploited by the rich.)

The wording of James 5:7—"Be patient, then, brothers"—seems to reflect a return to James' original audience: the Christian community. If this is the case, then James 5:7-11 is powerful encouragement for those being oppressed by the rich. This conclusion is supported by James' many references to perseverance in other parts of his letter.

Whether the rich in James 5 were within the Christian community or not, one thing is clear: their actions against the poor were wrong—a recurring theme throughout the letter. Take a minute to revisit the following verses. Note what you learn about the rich and the poor.

JAMES 1:9-11	JAMES 2:1-5	JAMES 4:13-14

What's the common theme in these passages?

_____

_____

Which group of people is commonly on the receiving end of James' instructions?

_____

SESSION

10

IT'S NOT
JUST THE
MONEY

JAMES
5:1-11

What's your account balance? Does it even matter?

James' strong language toward the rich indicates that God doesn't have much patience with the self-indulgent or those who hoard treasure. With God it's not the amount of wealth that's the problem but rather how the money is obtained and what's done with it after it's accumulated.

Note what you learn about the behavior God desires.

EXODUS 23:9

PSALM 82:1-4

MICAH 6:8

MATTHEW 5:7

LUKE 6:31-36

ROMANS 13:7-8

REFLECTION

Coming: a return on your investment

Review the instructions in James 5:7-11 that you listed on page 110. How do you characterize the type of behavior we're to have?

As you've probably noticed, James 5:1-11 consists of two segments—warnings to the rich and instructions for behavior. (The little word *then* in verse 7 ties these segments together.) Both of these segments are to be understood in light of the fact that Jesus' coming is near.

Prayerfully meditate about how these segments relate to one another. Factor in the things you learned about the Lord in this study. As the Spirit teaches you, journal below what comes to mind. Ask yourself, "What do I need to do in response to these verses?"

Share the wealth!

There are at least two good ways to apply this passage: as words of warning and as words of hope.

Words of Warning

You can be rich without having money. You can be rich in personality, in intelligence, in leadership, in initiative, and so on. And when we interact with people who aren't as rich as we are—in whatever area—our first impulse is often impatience. This may explain why James follows his assessment of the rich with admonitions of patience.

In which of the following areas do you consider yourself rich?

❏ friendships   ❏ decisiveness   ❏ common sense   ❏ planning

❏ intelligence   ❏ organization   ❏ problem solving   ❏ physical skill

❏ personality   ❏ vision   ❏ enthusiasm   ❏ self-motivation

How do you tend to react to those who are deficient in the areas where you're rich? If it's negatively, in what ways can your reaction have an oppressive effect on those people?

_____

_____

What can you do to share your riches?

_____

_____

What can you do to extend your patience?

_____

_____

What can you do to not "grumble"?

_____

_____

Words of Hope

James deals with perseverance through trials in the first chapter and now returns to it in the last chapter. If you've been doing this study at a rate of one session per week, it's been eight weeks since you studied James 1. You may be experiencing a completely different set of trials by now!

What circumstances are weighing heavy on your heart?

_____

_____

What situations are you or your friends experiencing that seem hopeless?

_____

_____

How's work? Do you feel exploited or oppressed?

_____

_____

SESSION
10

IT'S NOT
JUST THE
MONEY

JAMES
5:1-11

One of the most awesome themes of the New Testament is hope—specifically, the hope that no matter how tough this life may get, Jesus is coming back. Until his return, his grace and mercy—administered by the Holy Spirit—will comfort, restore, and preserve us. As you read the following passages, note the attitudes and actions we're to have in light of his imminent return. Take time to apply these to any of the situations you just listed.

1 CORINTHIANS 1:7-9

_____

_____

PHILIPPIANS 4:4-6

_____

_____

1 THESSALONIANS 5:22-23

_____

_____

HEBREWS 10:23-25

_____

_____

HEBREWS 10:34-37

_____

_____

REVELATION 22:20-21

_____

_____

CLOSING

Make a prayer deposit

Believers will experience Heaven—either when we die or when Jesus returns. And either of these events could happen sooner than we think. Before you meet with your students, give the Spirit an opportunity to impress upon you the reality of Heaven and the certainty of Christ's return. Trust the words of James and let your behavior reflect your dependence on God, rather than the wealth of this world.

Before you close this book be sure to read Teach It so you're comfortable with the flow of the session.

The format of Session 11 is different than the others and needs some advanced planning. If you

haven't already done so, look ahead now.

IT'S NOT JUST THE MONEY
James 5:1-11

SESSION
10

IT'S NOT
JUST THE
MONEY

JAMES
5:1-11

■ OPENING

This brainstorming exercise on money will lead the group into the subject of James 5.

■ SEARCH

Painting the money picture
Teens will discover words of warning for the rich and words of hope for the oppressed.

■ REFLECTION

Harsh words for the rich
This group discussion will help students understand that the words of warning in James 5 aren't only for people who are financially rich.

■ SOLITUDE

What's your account balance? Does it even matter?
Students see that the treatment of the poor is a subject close to God's heart.

■ APPLICATION

Share the wealth!
Students will work as a group to apply the words of warning and words of hope from James 5.

■ CLOSING

Make a prayer deposit
Closing in silent prayer will give students an opportunity to hear from and respond to God's Spirit.

YOU'LL NEED

a $10 or $20 bill

a whiteboard and markers

Bibles

pens

copies of It's Not Just the Money (pages 121-122), one for each student

copies of The Letter—James 5 (page 149), one for each student

colored pencils

OPENING

After the group has gathered, distribute materials and open with prayer. Let students discuss their applications from the last session.

Move into this session by holding up a $10 or $20 bill:

▸ *What I've got in my hand may look good to you, but it's something that can be used for good or for bad. How could it be used for bad?*

You can buy illegal vices with it (like prostitution or drugs).

You can buy destructive things with it (like pornography).

You can use its power to exploit people.

▸ *How can it be used for good?*

It could provide a meal or two for someone who's homeless.

You can buy a Bible or uplifting music with it.

You could put it toward sponsoring a child through a relief program.

Painting the money picture

▸ *Money is one of the top five topics addressed in Scripture. In fact, it gets almost as much attention as love. Read The Letter—James 5:1-11. As you read, circle every reference to the readers of the letter. In another color underline every reference to the Lord.*

After your kids have been working for about five minutes, ask—

▸ *What did you learn about the Lord in these verses?*

The cries of the harvesters have reached the ears of the Lord God (5:4).

The Lord Jesus is coming (5:7).

The Lord Jesus' coming is near (5:8).

The Lord God brought about great things in Job's life (5:11).

The Lord God is full of compassion and mercy (5:11).

List the students' observations on the board. Leave them on the board throughout the session. You'll come back to them. Help your group determine whether James is referring to Jesus or God with the title Lord.

▸ *What group of people does James appear to be singling out in this passage?*

The rich.

▶ *Can we draw any conclusions about who these rich people are in James 5:1-6? Are they the same people as in James 5:7-11?*

SESSION
10

IT'S NOT
JUST THE
MONEY

JAMES
5:1-11

As the students discuss, feel free to add your thoughts from your preparation time. Draw out the following possibilities:

— They could be rich people who are part of the Christian community (James' original audience).

— They could be rich people outside the Christian community who are exploiting James' readers. (See James 2:6.) In James 5:7-11 the author turns back to his original audience, the Christian community.

▶ *What word pictures does James use to describe the situation of the rich?*

Your wealth has rotted (5:2).

Moths have eaten your clothes (5:2).

The corrosion of your gold will eat your flesh like fire (5:3).

▶ *Why do you think James is being so harsh?*

The rich were exploiting their workers (the poor).

▶ *In verses 7-11, James instructs his readers about how they were to behave. Looking at what you circled in this passage, what behavior is James encouraging?*

Be patient (5:7).

Be patient and stand firm (5:8).

Don't grumble against each other (5:9).

▶ *Why were James' readers supposed to act this way?*

The Lord's coming is near (5:8).

Harsh words for the rich

▶ *Putting it all together, what two main points is James making in this passage?*

If you're rich, watch how you're using your riches! Don't exploit the poor.

If you're poor or being oppressed by those richer than you, be patient and persevere; the Lord is coming soon!

▶ *How do these teachings relate to the rest of James' letter?*

Encourage the students to look over The Letter from previous sessions. James addresses the subject of wealth in James 1:9-11; 2:1-9; and 4:13. Help the students see his pattern of defending the poor and admonishing the rich.

▶ *Which category do we fall into—the rich or the poor?*

There's no right or wrong answer to this question. Just help your teens relate their choice to James.

▶ *If we're not rich in money, there are ways we can still exploit people. All of us are rich in some way. We may be rich in personality, humor, athletic ability, or musical ability. Like money, all of these things can be used for bad or for good. For instance, how could you use humor to exploit people just as the rich exploited people in James 5?*

A person could use humor to humiliate someone or to get a laugh at another person's expense.

What's your account balance? Does it even matter?

Transition into the next exercise by saying—

▶ *If you've ever seen a homeless person and wondered if God cared, he does! In fact, God mentions the poor and the needy more than 200 times and in nearly every book of the Bible. In most of these verses God is asking his people (that means us) to look out for them.*

▶ *We won't be looking up all 200 verses, but I want to give you a chance to hear God's concern about helping people in need. So take your Bibles and handouts to a place where you have some privacy. As you read the passages listed in the first section of your handout, make notes on everything you learn about how we're to treat the needy.*

After about 10 minutes have your kids get back together.

▸ *How would you sum up the main theme of these verses?*

▸ *Any clues as to why mercy is such a big thing with God?*

SESSION
10

IT'S NOT
JUST THE
MONEY

JAMES
5:1-11

God wants us to show mercy to those who can't pay us back since God showed mercy to us and we can't ever pay him back. As we extend mercy, we show our gratitude for what God has done for us.

APPLICATION

Share the wealth!

▸ *There are two ways we can apply James 5:1-11—as a warning and as a declaration of hope. First let's look at the warning.*

The list about the Lord should still be on the board from earlier in the lesson. Direct your students back to it.

▸ *Let's get back to what we learned about the Lord in James 5:1-11. What trait of the Lord do you see that goes along with the Bible verses you just read?*

The Lord is full of compassion and mercy (5:11).

▸ *On your handout is a list of potential areas in which you could be rich—areas that have nothing to do with money. Check any that apply to you. Add other areas if you think of them.*

▸ *Then think about how can you use your riches to help those around you who are deficient or needy in the qualities in which you're rich. For example, if you circled intelligence, perhaps you could use your intelligence to tutor someone who struggles in that area. Write an idea or two for each quality you circled.*

After about five minutes have volunteers share their ideas.

▸ *On your copy of The Letter, look again at where you marked the instructions and references to the Lord in James 5:7-11. What connection do you see between these instructions and the info about the Lord?*

It's easier to be patient in suffering if you know that the Lord's coming soon. Patience and not grumbling are offshoots of compassion and mercy.

Ask three volunteers to look up these passages in their Bibles: Philippians 4:4-6, Hebrews 10:23-25, and Hebrews 10:34-37. While they're looking up the verses, say something like this:

> One of the main themes of the New Testament is, "Life as a believer will be tough, but take heart—Jesus is coming back!" We're going to listen to three Bible passages that reflect this theme. As each one is read, write any instructions you hear in the space provided on your handout.

Have the volunteers read the passages. Give your teens time to finish making notes between passages.

> How are these verses similar to James 5:7-11?

They give instructions for how we're to treat each other; they point to the fact that Jesus is coming soon.

As you ask the three primary questions below, have your teens rate themselves on the scales printed on their handouts. Accompanying each main question are a few related questions for discussion (not on the handout). If time allows, use these questions to help apply the three main points.

> *How well does your behavior toward others reflect the fact that Jesus could return any minute?*

> *How can your gentleness be evident to all?*

> *How can you encourage others and spur them on toward love and good deeds?*

> *How well does your behavior toward yourself reflect the fact that Jesus could return any minute?*

> *Are you persevering when times get tough?*

> *Are you overcoming temptation?*

> *Do you view your temptations in light of Jesus' return?*

> *How well does your behavior toward God reflect the fact that Jesus could return any minute?*

> *Do you pray as if he really exists?*

> *Do you try to get to know him as much as possible, so that you're familiar with him when you see him face to face?*

> *What are some ways you can celebrate God all day, every day?*

CLOSING

Make a prayer deposit

Spend the closing moments of the session in silent prayer. Ask the teens to dwell on the fact that Jesus is coming soon—maybe even tomorrow. Encourage them to think of their behavior in recent days—thoughts, attitudes, dates, free time, schoolwork—in light of the fact that Jesus could return sooner than they think. Allow several minutes of silent prayer, trusting that the Spirit will fill it with his voice.

In Session 11 some options for prayer on page 132 require advanced preparation. Take a look.

IT'S NOT JUST THE MONEY
James 5:1-11

SESSION
10

IT'S NOT
JUST THE
MONEY

JAMES
5:1-11

SOLITUDE

What's your account balance? Does it even matter?

As you read the following passages, make notes on everything you learn about how we're to treat the needy.

EXODUS 23:9

PSALM 82:1-4

_____

_____

MICAH 6:8

MATTHEW 5:7

_____

_____

LUKE 6:31-36

ROMANS 13:7-8

_____

_____

APPLICATION

Share the wealth!

Check the areas where you're rich. How can you use your riches to help others?

❏ friendships   ❏ common sense   ❏ self-motivation   ❏ vision   ❏ other

❏ intelligence   ❏ problem solving   ❏ decisiveness   ❏ planning

❏ personality   ❏ enthusiasm   ❏ organization   ❏ physical skill

Look up the following verses and write down the instructions we're given.

PHILIPPIANS 4:4-6

HEBREWS 10:23-25

_____

_____

How well does your behavior toward others reflect the fact that Jesus could return any minute?

I'm
embarrassed

I'm behaving
as Jesus would

How well does your behavior toward yourself reflect the fact that Jesus could return any minute?

I'm
embarrassed

I'm behaving
as Jesus would

How well does your behavior toward God reflect the fact that Jesus could return any minute?

I'm
embarrassed

I'm behaving
as Jesus would

LET'S DO PRAYER
James 5:12-18

Here's something you've got to see:

Very early in the morning, while it was still dark, Jesus got up, left the house and went off to a solitary place, where he prayed.

—Mark 1:35

But Jesus often withdrew to lonely places and prayed.

—Luke 5:16

One of those days Jesus went out to a mountainside to pray, and spent the night praying to God.
—Luke 6:12

About eight days after Jesus said this, he took Peter, John and James with him and went up onto a mountain to pray.

—Luke 9:28

One day Jesus was praying in a certain place...

—Luke 11:1

During the session with students, some options for prayer on page 132 require advanced preparation. Take a look now.

Jesus prayed early in the morning, throughout the night, by himself, with his friends, on a mountainside, in lonely places. And these are just a few of the times and places He prayed. Jesus couldn't wait to talk with the Father...anytime, anyplace.

Perhaps your prayer life has become haphazard—or even nonexistent. Today let Jesus' example and James' teaching move you to become a person of prayer...anytime, anyplace.

SEARCH

Everything you wanted to know about prayer

Read The Letter—James 5:12-18. As you read, circle every reference to prayer. After you've finished list every instruction concerning prayer.

Now list anything that gives insight into how you should pray. Look for things you're told to do, as well as descriptions about the intensity of prayer.

_____

_____

List the results of prayer that you find.

_____

_____

BACKGROUND

The mysterious land between prayer and healing

What about people we pray for who aren't healed? The session with your teens doesn't specifically cover this topic, but your kids may ask the question. To help you prepare for the group discussion, here are some points to consider as you study James 5.

Throughout Scripture, some sicknesses went unhealed.

—Paul prayed three times for his thorn in the flesh (possibly a physical ailment) to be removed. Paul was righteous and his prayer was fervent, yet the thorn was not removed (2 Corinthians 12:7-10).

—In 2 Timothy 4:20 Paul leaves his coworker Trophimus because he is sick. Certainly Paul and the apostles, prayer warriors all, would have prayed for his healing, yet Trophimus's illness disrupted his ministry with Paul.

—In many Scriptures, including James 1, we're told that sicknesses and hardships will come. Yet believers are encouraged to endure these trials, not expect them to be removed.

The phrase "offered in faith" is often misunderstood.

To offer a prayer in faith isn't the same as saying, "I really, really believe God's going to heal." The phrase offered in faith parallels Jesus' instruction to pray in his name and receive what we ask (see John 14:13; 15:16; 16:23). To pray in Jesus' name is to pray a prayer that Jesus would pray. Thus the prayer offered in faith is a prayer in accordance with God's will.

God can heal anyone at any time. When we offer our prayer in faith, we are submitting to God's sovereign will with the full knowledge that he can heal but that his ways and plans are higher than ours (Isaiah 55:9). The true prayer of faith joins Shadrach, Meshach, and Abednego in declaring, "The God we serve is able to save and rescue us. But even if he doesn't, our trust is in him alone!" (Daniel 3:17-18, paraphrased).

The phrase "will make the sick person well" may seem more definitive than it really is.

James' promise that the prayer offered in faith will make the sick person well doesn't leave much wiggle room for those who aren't made well. But even here there are some factors worth looking at.

First, the last half of this verse tells us how the sick person will be made well: the Lord will raise him up, and if he has sinned, he will be forgiven. This seems to point to a spiritual aspect of the healing, and in fact, the Greek word *sozo* can be translated "saved" or "healed."

Second, we're not given a clue as to the timing of the healing. It could be immediately after the prayer, at the time of Jesus' return, or after death.

The bottom line is that we can't manipulate the sovereignty of God. Perhaps the best way to understand this challenging passage is to focus on our part of the prayer process—and leave the results up to God.

APPLICATION

Shall we pray...

On that note let's assume that the most beneficial way to experience this passage is simply to do it—follow the steps and apply the actions James has given us, focusing on our responsibility in the prayer process.

What we should pray for

You listed situations we're to pray about when you were studying James 5:12-18. Now list anyone around you who falls into one of these categories—or anything you're personally experiencing that fits these descriptions.

_____

_____

Start with yourself

James hints that effective prayer begins with the inner life. Find the hints about our internal spiritual health in James 5:16 and write them below.

_____

_____

Has it ever occurred to you that an atmosphere of repentance and confession is the atmosphere most conducive to the mighty works of God? The great revivals of history ignited when God's people confessed and repented of their sins. Perhaps God is waiting for this atmosphere to be established in your student ministry or church. And perhaps it could begin with you.

Spend some time studying the following Bible verses. Look for the benefits of confession as well as any consequences of not confessing our sins.

2 CHRONICLES 7:13-15   *PROVERBS 28:13-14*

_____   _____

_____   _____

PSALM 51:1-10   *1 JOHN 1:9-10*

_____   _____

_____   _____

PSALM 66:16-20

_____

_____

What do you need to confess? Write it in code if you need to. Don't stop there. Carefully reread James 5:16, looking for what else (or who else) your confession should involve.

_____

_____

Show God you're serious

What are the practical steps James 5:12-18 gives to those preparing to offer a prayer in faith?

_____

_____

What are some ways your group or student ministry can apply the instruction to call the elders to pray?

_____

_____

If your church does not have designated elders or if your student ministry functions apart from a local church, how can you still apply the principles given in James? Remember, taking the Lord's instructions at face value shows him we're serious about obedience. Pray about what he would have your group do, then jot down your impressions.

_____

_____

Adopt the intensity

In verses 16 and 17 James gives a couple of clues about the level of prayer intensity God is looking for. Find these and write them down.

_____

_____

What needs to change in your prayer life so that it looks like the life of prayer James describes in these verses? Over the next two days, what can you give up, cancel, or reschedule to free up a block of time for earnest prayer?

_____

_____

CLOSING

Light the fire

Take God at his Word. Between now and the group session, dedicate yourself to praying the way James exhorts us to pray. Perhaps you and your students are to be the catalyst for establishing an atmosphere of physical and spiritual healing in your church or ministry. It all can start with you.

The structure of this session is different from previous sessions—it's a working prayer session. Be sure to read through the exercises—especially the options for prayer. Some of the options require advance planning. You may also want to confer with your pastor about any doctrines or beliefs held by your particular church or denomination that should be taught in the session.

SESSION 11

SESSION
11

LET'S DO
PRAYER

JAMES
5:12-18

SESSION 11

LET'S DO PRAYER
James 5:12-18

■OPENING

Get a glimpse of when, where, and how Jesus prayed.

■SEARCH

Everything you wanted to know about prayer
Students will observe in James the intensity required in prayer that produces results.

■REFLECTION

What are your prayers like?
This discussion helps teens evaluate their personal prayer intensity, as well as the overall intensity of prayer in their group or student ministry.

■APPLICATION

Shall we pray...
The backbone of this session is doing the kind of prayer James described.

■SOLITUDE

The Great 10-Minute Bible Study on Prayer
Your teens will consider the benefits of confession and the consequences of not confessing.

■CLOSING

Light the fire

■OPTION

This option gives students an opportunity to sing songs of praise as those who are happy are instructed to do in James 5:13.

■OPTION

This option gives students an opportunity to start looking for the rewards Scripture promises when they pursue a lifestyle of earnest prayer.

YOU'LL NEED

a whiteboard and markers

Bibles

pens

copies of Let's Do Prayer (pages 133-134), one for each student

copies of The Letter—James 5 (page 149), one for each new student

colored pencils

anointing oil (optional)

Students who were present for the last session should use the copies of James 5 they have already marked.

OPENING

After the group has gathered, distribute materials. Then ask volunteers to read the following Bible verses.

▸ *Before we pray, I want us to read some verses that show Jesus doing one of his favorite activities.*

▸ *Very early in the morning, while it was still dark, Jesus got up, left the house and went off to a solitary place, where he prayed.*

—Mark 1:35

▸ *But Jesus often withdrew to lonely places and prayed.*

—Luke 5:16

▸ *One of those days Jesus went out to a mountainside to pray, and spent the night praying to God.*

—Luke 6:12

▸ *About eight days after Jesus said this, he took Peter, John and James with him and went up onto a mountain to pray.*

—Luke 9:28

▸ *One day Jesus was praying in a certain place.*

—Luke 11:1

Feel free to share a few of your personal thoughts about these passages. Then open the session with prayer.

SEARCH

Everything you wanted to know about prayer

▸ *It's apparent that Jesus believes prayer is important, and as you'll see in a minute, James does, too. Read The Letter—James 5:12-18 and circle every mention of prayer.*

While the group reads and marks the passage, make three columns on the board. Label the columns: INSTRUCTIONS, HOW/INTENSITY, and RESULTS. After about five minutes, continue with the group—

▸ *Look at what you just marked and tell me any instructions we're given concerning prayer.*

You should pray if you're in trouble (5:13).

You should sing songs of praise if you're happy (5:13).

If you're sick, call the elders of the church to pray (5:14).

Confess your sins to each other and pray for each other (5:16).

As the students share, record their responses on the board in the first column.

▸ *What insight does James give as to how we should pray?*

Anoint the sick with oil in the name of the Lord (5:14).

Offer prayer in faith (5:15).

Make sure we're living a righteous life (5:16).

Confess our sins (5:16).

Pray earnestly, like Elijah (5:17).

As the students share, prompt them to look for things we're to do as well as for descriptions of the intensity we're to have. Record their responses on the board in the second column.

▸ *What results will we experience if we pray this way?*

The sick person will be made well (5:15).

The Lord will raise the sick person up (5:15).

His or her sins will be forgiven (5:15).

You will be healed (5:16).

It will be powerful and effective (5:16).

As the students share, record their responses on the board in the third column

REFLECTION

What are your prayers like?

Give the group a chance to process this information about prayer by discussing the questions below. Feel free to incorporate any insights from your preparation that will enhance their understanding.

▸ *When should we pray?*

When we're in trouble.   *When we're happy.*   *When we're sick.*

▸ *Do you think our prayer—as a student ministry—reflects the kind of prayer James was describing?*

▸ *Based on our current prayer life, do you think we can expect the results described in this passage?*

Transition into the next exercise by saying—

▸ *This passage may raise more questions than we can answer today, but one thing is sure. We've been given some specific things to focus on when it comes to our part of the prayer process. So let's focus on our half and let God take care of his half.*

APPLICATION

Shall we pray...

Turn the discussion to areas James suggests for prayer. Continue through the questions, allowing students time to share and to write down their requests. As group members share, encourage them to write each need in the space provided on their handouts. You can record them here for future follow-up.

▸ *Let's start with the things James tells us to pray for. Is anyone here in trouble? Are there areas of life that are especially tough right now? Are you experiencing any persecution because of your faith?*

> ▸ Is anyone happy? Has anything happened in your life that's given you peace?

> ▸ Is anyone sick? Do you know of friends or family members who are sick?

> ▸ Now let's concentrate on how we should pray. Look at the information in the column labeled HOW. Which of these items deals with our inner life?

Make sure we're living a righteous life (5:16).   Confess our sins (5:16).

Circle your teens' answers on the board and have them circle the choices on their handouts. Help them see that the kind of prayer God accepts and rewards does not begin with the words we say but with our inner spiritual life. The prayer God honors comes from an inner life that's been purified through confession and repentance and that seeks to live righteously.

> ▸ Did you know that God works in amazing ways when his people repent and confess their sins? The great spiritual revivals in history began when people repented wholeheartedly and asked God to clean them up. Maybe God is waiting on that kind of atmosphere in our church or student ministry before he'll move in the ways we've been asking him to. And maybe we could be the starting point!

SOLITUDE

The Great 10-Minute Bible Study on Prayer

Ask the students to move to a private place to do the exercise on their handouts. They'll also need to take their Bibles and pens. This part of the handout should look similar to this when the kids are finished.

SOLITUDE

The Great 10-Minute Bible Study on Prayer

Read the passages below from your Bible. As you read, jot down the benefits of confessing your sins. Also note any consequences you can expect when you don't confess your sins.

2 CHRONICLES 7:13-15

Benefits

God will hear from heaven, forgive sins, and heal our land.

PSALM 51:1-10

Benefits

We'll be clean. God will make us whiter than snow. We'll hear joy and gladness, our crushed bones will rejoice, and our iniquity will be blotted out.

PSALM 66:16-20

Consequences

The Lord will not listen if we cherish sin in our hearts.

Benefits

God listens and hears. He doesn't reject our prayer or withhold his love.

PROVERBS 28:13-14
Consequences

We won't prosper if we conceal our sin. We'll fall into trouble if we harden our hearts.

Benefits

We'll find mercy and be blessed.

1 JOHN 1:9-10
Consequences

If we claim we have not sinned, we make God out to be a liar, and his Word has no place in our lives.

Benefits

God is faithful to forgive our sins and purify us from all unrighteousness.

Take a few minutes to prayerfully read over the benefits and consequences you listed. What do you need to confess? What do you have in your life that you know is displeasing to God? Write it in code if necessary.

After about 15 minutes call your teens together.

▸ *You just spent time confessing your sins to God. But according to James, what else should we do?*

Confess our sins to each other (5:16).

Model a time of group confession for your students. As the leader you go first. Your ability to share openly will provide an example for those who are uncomfortable—perhaps that's all your teens. Help them see that everyone has sins to confess but that they can share in general terms if necessary, without offering a lot of embarrassing specifics. (They should only be confessing their own sins and not implicating others.)

Do not let this be a manipulative exercise. Be careful not to pressure students for details or wring confessions out of them. Let the Holy Spirit control the atmosphere and the sharing.

Let the kids know that if they have issues they need to discuss privately, you're available to talk with them after the session or at another time.

▸ *There are a few other things James says about how to pray. What other items on the board would indicate to God that we're taking prayer seriously?*

If you're sick, call the elders of the church to pray (5:14).

Anoint with oil in the name of the Lord (5:14).

Pray earnestly, like Elijah (5:17).

> ▸ On a scale from 1 (you're a prayer weakling) to 10 (you're a serious prayer warrior), how would you rate your method of praying over the last 10 days?

> ▸ What are some things we can do to pray earnestly and show God that we take prayer seriously?

Keep a prayer journal.

Establish a prayer corner, prayer chair, or prayer closet.

Spend scheduled prayer time when you're most alert. (This doesn't preclude praying as you go about your day.)

Assume a posture of humility, such as kneeling, during prayer.

You've identified things to pray for, confessed your sins to one another, and observed the level of intensity God desires. Now allow some group time to pray for the troubles and sicknesses shared earlier in the session. Here are some suggestions for how the group might pray.

Call the elders

If any of your students are sick, you may want to invite the elders of your church to the study session. Since the sick are the people to call the elders, be sure to speak with the ill student in advance. If your church doesn't have elders, perhaps you and some of your adult or student leaders can serve as elders.

Anoint with oil

The oil referred to in James 5:14 was probably olive oil, which can be found in any grocery store. Traditions vary, but one method is to dab a finger in the oil and trace the shape of the cross on the forehead of the person being anointed.

You may want to pour the oil into a vial and use the vial for this exercise. Check with your pastor or purchase one at a Christian bookstore. Again, if your church doesn't designate elders, you and other group leaders can anoint the sick with oil.

Adopt a prayer posture in solitude

The students may prefer to pray by themselves rather than as a group. If so, invite them to take their handouts from this session so they can pray about the needs discussed earlier in the session. Encourage them to adopt a prayer posture (such as kneeling at the seat of a chair, kneeling facedown, or lying facedown on the floor).

Adopt a prayer posture as a group

Invite the teens to kneel at their chairs or on the floor. Spend some time in silence, letting the students pray for the needs expressed earlier. Then ask them to pray aloud as they feel led.

CLOSING

Light the fire

OPTION

If your group has not addressed singing songs of praise when anyone is happy (James 5:13), you may want to close the session doing just that. Ask the students to suggest songs that go along with the praiseworthy events they listed on the handout earlier.

OPTION

James mentions some powerful promises we can enjoy if we pray as he instructed. Ask the students to use this session's handout as their first entry in a prayer journal. Challenge them to keep track of the people and situations listed in the chart on pages 128-129. Remind them to expect healing, forgiveness, power, and impact.

LET'S DO PRAYER

James 5:12-18

APPLICATION

Shall we pray...

Write down requests for prayer suggested by group members.

Trouble

Happy

Sick

Inner life of prayer

SOLITUDE

The Great 10-Minute Bible Study on Prayer

Read the passages below from your Bible. As you read, jot down the benefits of confessing your sins. Also note any consequences you can expect when you don't confess your sins.

2 CHRONICLES 7:13-15
Benefits

PSALM 51:1-10
Benefits

PSALM 66:16-20
Consequences

_____

_____

Benefits

_____

_____

PROVERBS 28:13-14
Consequences

_____

_____

Benefits

_____

_____

1 JOHN 1:9-10
Consequences

_____

_____

Benefits

_____

_____

Take a few minutes to prayerfully read over the benefits and consequences you listed. What do you need to confess? What do you have in your life that you know is displeasing to God? Write it in code if necessary.

SESSION
12

TOTAL
TURN-
AROUND

JAMES
5:19-20

TOTAL TURNAROUND
James 5:19-20

The Sadducees were a Jewish sect prominent in Jesus' day who didn't believe in the resurrection or life after death. Knowing that Jesus was not only claiming to be the Son of God, but also trumpeting the promise of eternal life, the Sadducees felt threatened. They figured that if they could embarrass Jesus and unravel his claims by throwing him a stumper question in front of a large crowd, they'd never hear from him again. So they pulled together their brightest minds and presented their best airtight, faith-unraveling question (about marriage in heaven). Read how Jesus began his response below, along with the reaction of the dumbstruck crowd.

Jesus replied, "You are in error because you do not know the Scriptures or the power of God."
—Matthew 22:29

When the crowds heard this, they were astonished at his teaching.
—Matthew 22:33

The Sadducees failed to accomplish their mission—and Jesus nailed the reason for their error. Are we different from the Sadducees today? Even among believers, plans fail, energy is wasted, and misguided decisions are made because people know neither the Scriptures nor the power of God.

Scholar Douglas J. Moo in *The Letter of James, The Pillar New Testament Commentary* (2000) asserts that the book of James contains more imperatives (direct commands and instructions) per word than any other New Testament book. It's fitting then that James closes his letter not with gushy goodbyes but with pragmatic instructions to help believers stay close to the truth and experience the power of God.

Wandering and wanderers

Using The Letter, read James 5:19-20. Mark the two types of people represented in the passage. (You might circle one and underline the other.) Then write in the spaces below a description of the two types of people you identified. Reread James 5:19-20 and list everything you learn about each type of person.

Think for a moment about what it might look like to "wander from the truth." Write four or five actions that might indicate that someone is wandering from the truth.

If you begin to notice such actions in Christians, what are some ways you could help "turn a sinner from the error of his way"? Write four or five ideas below.

The Bible as guardrail

Scripture gives us some red flags that can indicate when someone we know is wandering from the truth, as well as tips on how to turn a sinner from error. As you read the following Bible verses, write what you learn about how someone can stray from the truth.

EXODUS 23:2

JUDGES 2:10-12

PSALM 119:10-11

LUKE 21:8

JAMES 1:13-18

JAMES 3:14

As you read the next set of passages, record what you learn about why we should bother helping someone who has strayed from the truth. If you learn anything new about how a person might wander, add this information too.

EZEKIEL 34:1-4, 10
(Though this passage is aimed at the shepherds of Israel, every spiritual leader and discipler can take its message to heart.)

MATTHEW 18:15-20

1 PETER 4:8-11

SESSION

12

TOTAL
TURN-
AROUND

JAMES
5:19-20

JUDE 21-23

REFLECTION

Why leave the path?

Let's put it all together. Based on the first set of verses you read, summarize the variety of ways people can wander from the truth.

Based on the second set of verses, summarize how we should proceed in helping the wanderer return to the path.

APPLICATION

Any wanderers you know?

You probably noticed that the wanderers James' readers were to look after were those in the Christian community ("My brothers, if one of you should wander…"). Think for a moment about the students who are currently involved with your ministry. In the first column write the names or initials of students who are exhibiting any of the red flags you saw in the Bible verses you looked up earlier. Also consider any teens who were once part of your flock but who have recently gravitated away.

Students	Steps toward restoration

Now prayerfully run each name through the scriptural steps for bringing a wanderer back to truth. Ask God for wisdom—which he gives generously—in applying these steps to each unique situation. In the second column write practical actions you can take to begin the process of restoration.

CLOSING

Reach out and review

In the group session your students will also be asked to think about any peers who are wandering from the truth. As you and the group work through this exercise, be open to letting a plan emerge that will help you be intentional in reaching out to those who have gravitated to the fringes of your ministry.

Since this is the last session in your study of James, you'll want to devote a few minutes to a review of the group's experience in James.

TOTAL TURNAROUND
James 5:19-20

SESSION
12

TOTAL
TURN-
AROUND

JAMES
5:19-20

■ OPENING

This brainstorming exercise will introduce the subject of the session: restoring those who depart from the truth.

■ SEARCH

Wandering and wanderers

Students will discover the type of person James has in mind as he brings his letter to a close.

■ REFLECTION

What does wandering look like?

This group discussion will help students see how relevant James' concern is today.

■ SOLITUDE

The Bible as guardrail

This solitude exercise allows students to check out key Scriptures that give added insight on how to respond when friends wander from the truth.

■ REFLECTION

Why leave the path?

This group discussion will help students think in more practical terms about what they learned during the Solitude exercise.

■ APPLICATION

Any wanderers you know?

Students will apply James' closing concerns to the people in their spheres of contact.

■ RECAP

So how was the trip?

This exercise will give the group time to reflect on and share about the impact of James on their lives.

> **YOU'LL NEED**
>
> *a whiteboard and markers*
>
> *Bibles*
>
> *pens*
>
> *copies of Total Turnaround (page 145), one for each student*
>
> *copies of The Letter—James 5 (page 149), one for each new student*
>
> *colored pencils*
>
> *blank paper (optional)*

OPENING

After the group has gathered, distribute materials and open with prayer. Ask again about applications from previous lessons.

Begin the session with this brainstorming exercise. Ask—

▸ When people walk away from faith in God, what are some reasons they give?

Christians are hypocrites.

There's too much fighting in the church.

If a loving God is in control, why is there so much suffering?

The only thing the church wants is money.

▸ What do you think about these reasons? (Respond in general terms, not to each specific question.)

Wandering and wanderers

▸ Just because James' readers were receiving a letter that would eventually become part of the Bible doesn't mean that everything was perfect in their world. In a minute we'll see that they experienced something we also find disheartening—watching their friends walk away from God.

▸ In James 5:19-20 we find two types of people. As you read this passage using *The Letter*, find these two types of people. Underline references to one type and circle references to the other type.

After the kids have been working for about five minutes, ask—

▸ What are the two types of people in this passage?

The one who wanders from the truth

The one who turns a sinner from the error of his way

Why leave the path?

▸ What does wandering look like?

▸ Just by reading James 5, what do we know about the one who wanders?

The wanderer is part of the Christian community.

The wanderer must have embraced the truth at one time.

The wanderer is wandering from what he embraced.

The wanderer is in error.

The wanderer is headed toward death.

▸ What do we know about the one who turns the sinner around?

He will save the brother from death.

He will cover a multitude of sins.

SESSION
12

TOTAL
TURN-
AROUND

JAMES
5:19-20

▸ *Think about the phrase "wander from the truth." In practical terms, what might that look like?*

Giving in to temptations

Choosing to live a rebellious lifestyle

Distancing oneself from Christian influences like church, youth group, Christian friends, etc.

Making choices with no regard for God's consequences

Consciously deciding to believe that God does not exist

Consciously deciding that truth is whatever you want it to be

▸ *What might it look like to "turn a sinner from the error of his way"?*

Living in a way that shows God's truth to be an incredible thing to give your life to.

Being able to gently and tactfully point out bad decisions and judgments.

Not giving up on a friend who is wandering.

SOLITUDE

The Bible as guardrail

▸ *We're going to spend some time letting God's Word answer the last two questions we just discussed. Take your handouts and your Bibles to a place of privacy and do the exercise titled The Bible as Guardrail printed on your handout.*

REFLECTION

Why leave the path?

After about 15 minutes, call the group back together.

▸ *Based on these passages what are some ways people can wander from the truth?*

People follow the crowd in doing wrong (Exodus 23:2).

Parents don't tell the next generation about God, so kids don't know about God and wander from their parents' faith (Judges 2:10)

People follow and worship gods of the people around them (false religions and other forms of idolatry) (Judges 2:12).

They stray away from the commands of God in his Word (Psalm 119:10).

They don't really seek him or hide his Word in their hearts (Psalm 119:10-11).

They are deceived by others who speak a twisted version of the truth (Luke 21:8).

They're enticed by their own evil desires, which progressively lead to death (James 1:14-15).

They harbor bitter envy and selfish ambition (James 3:14).

Write the responses on the left half of the board.

▸ *How have you seen these ways draw people away from the truth today?*

▸ *Based on the passages about turning a sinner from the error of his way, what steps would you take to help turn a friend back to the truth?*

If they've been wounded, find ways to strengthen, heal, and bind them up (Ezekiel 34:1-4).

Go after the strays; don't wait till they come to you (Ezekiel 34:1-4).

Take care of the flock, not just yourself (Ezekiel 34:1-4).

Try the one-on-one approach before bringing in other help (Matthew 18:15-17).

Love deeply; serve others (1 Peter 4:8).

Administer God's grace using whatever gifts you've been given (1 Peter 4:10).

When in doubt about what to say, use God's words (1 Peter 4:11).

Be merciful to those who doubt (Jude 21-23).,

Write their responses on the right half of the board. Remind the group that one of the best ways to keep people from wandering from the truth is for God's people to know truth and live it. (Isn't that what the book of James is all about?) In most cases when people stray from God, it's not truth they're rejecting but a poor projection of truth shown by the Christians around them.

Truth is the antidote to deception—and many of the things that draw people away from truth are based on deception (temptations, false religions, worldly philosophies). The better we know truth and live it, the less susceptible we are to temptation and deception.

APPLICATION

Who can you restore?

▸ *We've looked at several ways that people can wander from the truth. Now take a minute to think about the people you know. In the space provided on your handout, jot the names or initials of those you know who may be wandering from the truth. Remember that James was talking about people who are part of the Christian community.*

After a couple of minutes, ask—

▸ *Now think about two or three things you could do for each person that could help turn them from the error of their ways. Base your actions on the passages you just read during Solitude.*

Have the students write these ideas in the space provided on their handouts.

▸ *What were some of your ideas for helping restore your friends to the truth?*

SESSION
12

TOTAL
TURN-
AROUND

JAMES
5:19-20

Listen more to their concerns.

Establish a caring relationship before barging in with help.

Show mercy to those who've made bad decisions.

Know truth myself (spend time in God's Word).

Pray for them.

Talk one on one and ask the hard questions with love.

Encourage the students to hold one another accountable to implement these ideas with the friends and family members they listed. Remind them to pray for these people and count on the Holy Spirit to help bring them back.

Close the discussion by having your teenagers consider this question:

▸ *Why do you think James ends his letter with the subject of turning a wanderer back to the truth?*

Since James is so action oriented, it's appropriate that the author's final encouragement is about keeping believers connected to the truth. That's where we receive the power and motivation to do all the other actions James addresses in his letter.

RECAP

So how was the trip?

Since this is the group's final session in James, spend some time reviewing the book as a whole. Listed below are some questions to use as a guide. You may want to appoint a scribe to record the students' thoughts and convictions as they share. As a follow-up to the study, provide a copy of these responses to group members.

▸ *How have you changed as a result of studying the book of James—*

▸ *in your attitudes toward those around you?*

▸ *in your actions toward people in need?*

▸ *in your understanding of God?*

▸ *in your relationship with Jesus?*

▸ *What instruction was the most convicting or challenging?*

▸ *What was your biggest "Wow!" moment?*

▸ *If you were to retitle the book of James (possibly with a more descriptive title), what would you call it?*

TOTAL TURNAROUND
James 5:19-20

SESSION
12
TOTAL
TURN-
AROUND

JAMES
5:19-20

SOLITUDE

The Bible as guardrail

What might it look like to "wander from the truth"?

As you read the following Bible verses from your Bible, pay close attention to how a person can wander away from God. Write down what you learn about how and why people stray from the truth.

EXODUS 23:2

JUDGES 2:10-12

PSALM 119:10-11

LUKE 21:8

JAMES 1:13-18

JAMES 3:14

What might it look like to "turn a sinner from the error of his way"?

As you read the next set of Bible verses, write anything you learn about how or why we should bother helping someone who's strayed from the truth.

EZEKIEL 34:1-4, 10

MATTHEW 18:15-20

1 PETER 4:8-11

JUDE 21-23

APPLICATION

Any wanderers you know?

Write down the names or initials of people you know who may be wandering from the truth and jot down ideas for helping restore your friends to the truth.

THE LETTER
James 1

1 James, a servant of God and of the Lord Jesus Christ, To the twelve tribes scattered among the nations: Greetings.

2 Consider it pure joy, my brothers, whenever you face trials of many kinds,

3 because you know that the testing of your faith develops perseverance.

4 Perseverance must finish its work so that you may be mature and complete, not lacking anything.

5 If any of you lacks wisdom, he should ask God, who gives generously to all without finding fault, and it will be given to him.

6 But when he asks, he must believe and not doubt, because he who doubts is like a wave of the sea, blown and tossed by the wind.

7 That man should not think he will receive anything from the Lord;

8 he is a double-minded man, unstable in all he does.

9 The brother in humble circumstances ought to take pride in his high position.

10 But the one who is rich should take pride in his low position, because he will pass away like a wild flower.

11 For the sun rises with scorching heat and withers the plant; its blossom falls and its beauty is destroyed. In the same way, the rich man will fade away even while he goes about his business.

12 Blessed is the man who perseveres under trial, because when he has stood the test, he will receive the crown of life that God has promised to those who love him.

13 When tempted, no one should say, "God is tempting me." For God cannot be tempted by evil, nor does he tempt anyone;

14 but each one is tempted when, by his own evil desire, he is dragged away and enticed.

15 Then, after desire has conceived, it gives birth to sin; and sin, when it is full-grown, gives birth to death.

16 Don't be deceived, my dear brothers.

17 Every good and perfect gift is from above, coming down from the Father of the heavenly lights, who does not change like shifting shadows.

18 He chose to give us birth through the word of truth, that we might be a kind of firstfruits of all he created.

19 My dear brothers, take note of this: Everyone should be quick to listen, slow to speak and slow to become angry,

20 for man's anger does not bring about the righteous life that God desires.

21 Therefore, get rid of all moral filth and the evil that is so prevalent and humbly accept the word planted in you, which can save you.

22 Do not merely listen to the word, and so deceive yourselves. Do what it says.

23 Anyone who listens to the word but does not do what it says is like a man who looks at his face in a mirror

24 and, after looking at himself, goes away and immediately forgets what he looks like.

25 But the man who looks intently into the perfect law that gives freedom, and continues to do this, not forgetting what he has heard, but doing it—he will be blessed in what he does.

26 If anyone considers himself religious and yet does not keep a tight rein on his tongue, he deceives himself and his religion is worthless.

27 Religion that God our Father accepts as pure and faultless is this: to look after orphans and widows in their distress and to keep oneself from being polluted by the world.

THE LETTER
James 2

1 My brothers, as believers in our glorious Lord Jesus Christ, don't show favoritism.

2 Suppose a man comes into your meeting wearing a gold ring and fine clothes, and a poor man in shabby clothes also comes in.

3 If you show special attention to the man wearing fine clothes and say, "Here's a good seat for you," but say to the poor man, "You stand there" or "Sit on the floor by my feet,"

4 have you not discriminated among yourselves and become judges with evil thoughts?

5 Listen, my dear brothers: Has not God chosen those who are poor in the eyes of the world to be rich in faith and to inherit the kingdom he promised those who love him?

6 But you have insulted the poor. Is it not the rich who are exploiting you? Are they not the ones who are dragging you into court?

7 Are they not the ones who are slandering the noble name of him to whom you belong?

8 If you really keep the royal law found in Scripture, "Love your neighbor as yourself," you are doing right.

9 But if you show favoritism, you sin and are convicted by the law as lawbreakers.

10 For whoever keeps the whole law and yet stumbles at just one point is guilty of breaking all of it.

11 For he who said, "Do not commit adultery," also said, "Do not murder." If you do not commit adultery but do commit murder, you have become a lawbreaker.

12 Speak and act as those who are going to be judged by the law that gives freedom,

13 because judgment without mercy will be shown to anyone who has not been merciful. Mercy triumphs over judgment!

14 What good is it, my brothers, if a man claims to have faith but has no deeds? Can such faith save him?

15 Suppose a brother or sister is without clothes and daily food.

16 If one of you says to him, "Go, I wish you well; keep warm and well fed," but does nothing about his physical needs, what good is it?

17 In the same way, faith by itself, if it is not accompanied by action, is dead.

18 But someone will say, "You have faith; I have deeds." Show me your faith without deeds, and I will show you my faith by what I do.

19 You believe that there is one God. Good! Even the demons believe that—and shudder

20 You foolish man, do you want evidence that faith without deeds is useless?

21 Was not our ancestor Abraham considered righteous for what he did when he offered his son Isaac on the altar?

22 You see that his faith and his actions were working together, and his faith was made complete by what he did.

23 And the scripture was fulfilled that says, "Abraham believed God, and it was credited to him as righteousness," and he was called God's friend.

24 You see that a person is justified by what he does and not by faith alone.

25 In the same way, was not even Rahab the prostitute considered righteous for what she did when she gave lodging to the spies and sent them off in a different direction?

26 As the body without the spirit is dead, so faith without deeds is dead.

THE LETTER
James 3

1 Not many of you should presume to be teachers, my brothers, because you know that we who teach will be judged more strictly.

2 We all stumble in many ways. If anyone is never at fault in what he says, he is a perfect man, able to keep his whole body in check.

3 When we put bits into the mouths of horses to make them obey us, we can turn the whole animal.

4 Or take ships as an example. Although they are so large and are driven by strong winds, they are steered by a very small rudder wherever the pilot wants to go.

5 Likewise the tongue is a small part of the body, but it makes great boasts. Consider what a great forest is set on fire by a small spark.

6 The tongue also is a fire, a world of evil among the parts of the body. It corrupts the whole person, sets the whole course of his life on fire, and is itself set on fire by hell.

7 All kinds of animals, birds, reptiles and creatures of the sea are being tamed and have been tamed by man,

8 but no man can tame the tongue. It is a restless evil, full of deadly poison.

9 With the tongue we praise our Lord and Father, and with it we curse men, who have been made in God's likeness.

10 Out of the same mouth come praise and cursing. My brothers, this should not be.

11 Can both fresh water and salt water flow from the same spring?

12 My brothers, can a fig tree bear olives, or a grapevine bear figs? Neither can a salt spring produce fresh water.

13 Who is wise and understanding among you? Let him show it by his good life, by deeds done in the humility that comes from wisdom.

14 But if you harbor bitter envy and selfish ambition in your hearts, do not boast about it or deny the truth.

15 Such "wisdom" does not come down from heaven but is earthly, unspiritual, of the devil.

16 For where you have envy and selfish ambition, there you find disorder and every evil practice.

17 But the wisdom that comes from heaven is first of all pure; then peace-loving, considerate, submissive, full of mercy and good fruit, impartial and sincere.

18 Peacemakers who sow in peace raise a harvest of righteousness.

THE LETTER
James 4

1 What causes fights and quarrels among you? Don't they come from your desires that battle within you?

2 You want something but don't get it. You kill and covet, but you cannot have what you want. You quarrel and fight. You do not have, because you do not ask God.

3 When you ask, you do not receive, because you ask with wrong motives, that you may spend what you get on your pleasures.

4 You adulterous people, don't you know that friendship with the world is hatred toward God? Anyone who chooses to be a friend of the world becomes an enemy of God.

5 Or do you think Scripture says without reason that the spirit he caused to live in us envies intensely?

6 But he gives us more grace. That is why Scripture says: "God opposes the proud but gives grace to the humble."

7 Submit yourselves, then, to God. Resist the devil, and he will flee from you.

8 Come near to God and he will come near to you. Wash your hands, you sinners, and purify your hearts, you double-minded.

9 Grieve, mourn and wail. Change your laughter to mourning and your joy to gloom.

10 Humble yourselves before the Lord, and he will lift you up.

11 Brothers, do not slander one another. Anyone who speaks against his brother or judges him speaks against the law and judges it. When you judge the law, you are not keeping it, but sitting in judgment on it.

12 There is only one Lawgiver and Judge, the one who is able to save and destroy. But you—

who are you to judge your neighbor?

13 Now listen, you who say, "Today or tomorrow we will go to this or that city, spend a year there, carry on business and make money."

14 Why, you do not even know what will happen tomorrow. What is your life? You are a mist that appears for a little while and then vanishes.

15 Instead, you ought to say, "If it is the Lord's will, we will live and do this or that."

16 As it is, you boast and brag. All such boasting is evil.

17 Anyone, then, who knows the good he ought to do and doesn't do it, sins.

THE LETTER
James 5

1 Now listen, you rich people, weep and wail because of the misery that is coming upon you.

2 Your wealth has rotted, and moths have eaten your clothes.

3 Your gold and silver are corroded. Their corrosion will testify against you and eat your flesh like fire. You have hoarded wealth in the last days.

4 Look! The wages you failed to pay the workmen who mowed your fields are crying out against you. The cries of the harvesters have reached the ears of the Lord Almighty.

5 You have lived on earth in luxury and self-indulgence. You have fattened yourselves in the day of slaughter.

6 You have condemned and murdered innocent men, who were not opposing you.

7 Be patient, then, brothers, until the Lord's coming. See how the farmer waits for the land to yield its valuable crop and how patient he is for the autumn and spring rains.

8 You too, be patient and stand firm, because the Lord's coming is near.

9 Don't grumble against each other, brothers, or you will be judged. The Judge is standing at the door!

10 Brothers, as an example of patience in the face of suffering, take the prophets who spoke in the name of the Lord.

11 As you know, we consider blessed those who have persevered. You have heard of Job's perseverance and have seen what the Lord finally brought about. The Lord is full of compassion and mercy.

12 Above all, my brothers, do not swear—not by heaven or by earth or by anything else. Let your "Yes" be yes, and your "No," no, or you will be condemned.

13 Is any one of you in trouble? He should pray. Is anyone happy? Let him sing songs of praise.

14 Is any one of you sick? He should call the elders of the church to pray over him and anoint him with oil in the name of the Lord.

15 And the prayer offered in faith will make the sick person well; the Lord will raise him up. If he has sinned, he will be forgiven.

16 Therefore confess your sins to each other and pray for each other so that you may be healed. The prayer of a righteous man is powerful and effective.

17 Elijah was a man just like us. He prayed earnestly that it would not rain, and it did not rain on the land for three and a half years.

18 Again he prayed, and the Heavens gave rain, and the earth produced its crops.

19 My brothers, if one of you should wander from the truth and someone should bring him back,

20 remember this: Whoever turns a sinner from the error of his way will save him from death and cover over a multitude of sins.

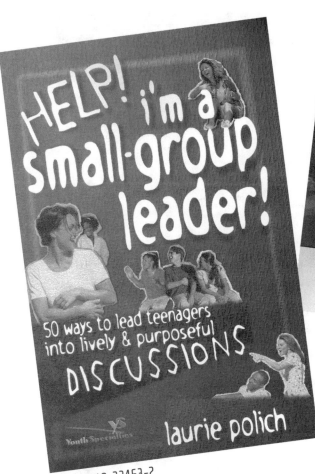